CHINUA ACHEBE, the distinguished Nigerian writer, and C. L. INNES a lecturer and literary critic on African and Caribbean literature, have collaborated in selecting and introducing this anthology of short stories which represent the excellence of African writing over the last 30 years.

CHINUA ACHEBE has taught at the Universities of Nigeria, Massachussetts and Connecticut and among the many honours he has received in recognition of his contribution to contemporary literature he holds the Fellowship of the Modern Language Association of America and doctorates from the Universities of Stirling, Southampton and Kent. His best-selling, classic novel *Things Fall Apart*, first published in 1958, has now sold over two million copies and been translated into over 30 languages. His later novels, short stories and poems have earned him numerous prizes including the Commonwealth Poetry Prize and the Scottish Arts Council Neil Gunn Fellowship. He is editor of *Okike: An African Journal of New Writing*, founded in 1971.

C. L. INNES has taught English and comparative literature at universities in Australia, the United States and England, where she currently lectures at the University of Kent. She has co-edited *Critical Perspectives on Chinua Achebe* (Heinemann) and published a number of articles on African and Irish literature. Her latest work on the subject is *The Devil's Own Mirror: a Comparative Study on Irish and African Literature* (Three Continents Press, Washington D.C.).

SELECTED AND EDITED BY

CHINUA ACHEBE
and C. L. INNES

AFRICAN
SHORT STORIES

HEINEMANN

Heinemann International Literature and Textbooks
a division of Heinemann Educational Books Ltd
Halley Court, Jordan Hill, Oxford OX2 8EJ

Heinemann Educational Books Inc
361 Hanover Street, Portsmouth, New Hampshire, 03801, USA

Heinemann Educational Books (Nigeria) Ltd
PMB 5205, Ibadan
Heinemann Kenya Ltd
PO Box 45314, Nairobi, Kenya
Heinemann Educational Boleswa
PO Box 10103, Village Post Office, Gaborone, Botswana

LONDON EDINBURGH MELBOURNE SYDNEY
AUCKLAND SINGAPORE TOKYO MADRID
PARIS ATHENS BOLOGNA HARARE

AWS Series Editor: Adewale Maja-Pearce

British Library Cataloguing in Publication Data

African short stories.—(African writers series).
1. Short Stories, African (English)
I. Achebe, Chinua   II. Innes, C. L.   III. Series
823'01'0896[FS]   PR9347.5

ISBN 0-435-90536-8

Printed in Great Britain by
Cox & Wyman Ltd, Reading, Berkshire

92 93 94 95 10 9 8 7 6

CONTENTS

Introduction

The short story has enjoyed the attention and patronage of African writers from Peter Abrahams' 1942 collection, *Dark Testament*, to the present time. One can recognize this long-standing popularity of the genre without accepting one foreign critic's silly notion that the short story was native to Africa and therefore strong whereas the novel was alien and therefore weak!

This anthology makes the assumption that *story* is not necessarily *short story*, a modern form of short fiction actually younger than the novel.

Both novel and short story in Africa have undoubtedly drawn from a common oral heritage. But each has also achieved distinctiveness in the hands of its best practitioners. Jomo Kenyatta's *Gentlemen of the Jungle*, which on account of its time and circumstance might have been expected to manifest strong transitional traits, is actually no moonlight tale but one of the most successfully realized modern examples in the anthology.

The indebtedness of modern African writing to its wealth of oral traditions is taken for granted by the editors and they see no necessity to demonstrate the link further by including traditional tales in this collection. Also, in a situation where only a small number from a large and growing body of good short stories can be presented they had perforce to rule against the inclusion of extracts from novels.

The rich contrasts of Africa are well displayed in this book— stories of the north, spare as Islamic calligraphy beside the more densely and luxuriantly realized species from further south; the marginality of racial themes—verging almost on complacency—on the west coast, and the painful inescapable bond to racism in the south. But equally (or perhaps, more) striking is a certain spirit of unity which is more than a political cliché. Though the backdrops are so different, for example, in Alifa Rifaat and Ama Ata Aidoo, their stories north and south of the Sahara recount synoptically the ageless solidarity of suffering which a mother offers her daughter as she comes face to face for the first time with the threat and betrayal that will be her lot in a man's world.

Although the editors were mindful of the advantages of representing writers of different regions, sexes and generations in this anthology, their criterion was ultimately literary merit. And as it turned out their selections went ahead with gratifying serendipity to meet the other considerations as well! The subsequent grouping of the stories into broad geographical regions seemed a handy and practical arrangement. But any other format might have done just as well: we might have arranged the authors alphabetically or the stories chronologically, and so on.

I commend this book to lovers of good writing in Africa and elsewhere. In putting it together we had in mind to appeal to the general reader. But my own experience from teaching African fiction for a few years at the University of Nigeria, Nsukka, had shown me that a majority of students came to the course with a poor background of reading and consequently tended to be intimidated by the sheer size of the novels they had to study. One way I found to alleviate their terror was to begin each course with the study of half-a-dozen or so African short stories. I hope that other students and other teachers will find this anthology a manageable and enjoyable introduction into the art and the world of African fiction.

Chinua Achebe
University of Guelph
Ontario, Canada
May 1984

Notes on Contributors

Chinua Achebe was born in Ogidi, Eastern Nigeria in 1930. He is the author of four novels, *Things Fall Apart*, *No Longer At Ease*, *Arrow of God*, and *A Man of the People*. He has also published a volume of short stories, *Girls At War and Other Stories* and a volume of poetry, *Beware Soul Brother*.

Ama Ata Aidoo (born 1940) is one of Ghana's best known writers. In addition to the plays *Anowa* and *Dilemma of a Ghost*, she has published a novel, *Our Sister Killjoy*, and a collection of short stories, *No Sweetness Here*.

Odun Balogun teaches English at the University of Benin, Nigeria.

Mohamed El-Bisatie (born 1938) has worked as a government official in Egypt. He has published two volumes of short stories and a novel in Arabic.

Ahmed Essop has been publishing stories about the Indian community in Johannesburg since 1969. His collection, *The Hajji and Other Stories*, won the Olive Schreiner Award in 1979.

Nadine Gordimer (born 1923) has published more than a dozen short-story collections and novels, most of which are set in her native South Africa. She shared the Booker Prize (UK) for her novel *The Conservationist* in 1975, and was also awarded the French International Literary Prize, Le Grand Aigle d'Or, that year. Her most recent novel is *July's People* (1981).

Abdulrazak Gurnah was born in 1948 and educated in Tanzania. He is the author of two novels and currently works in London.

Mafika Gwala was born in Verulam, South Africa in 1946, and has worked as a clerk, teacher, factory worker and publications researcher. He edited *Black Review 1973*, has published articles, stories and a book of poems, *Jol'iinkomo*.

Bessie Head was born in Pietermaritzburg, South Africa in 1937. She has published three novels, *When Rain Clouds Gather*, *Maru* and *A Question of Power*, and a volume of short stories, *The Collector of Treasures*, all of which are set in Botswana where she now lives in exile. Her latest book, *Serowe Village of the Rain-Wind* reconstructs the social history of an African community.

Luis Bernardo Honwana (born 1943) grew up in Moambo, Mozambique, and began publishing stories at the age of seventeen. During the war of liberation he served a political prison sentence, and since independence he has worked for the new administration. His collection, *We Killed Mangy Dog and Other Stories* was translated from the Portuguese and published in 1969.

Jomo Kenyatta (1891–1978) became Kenya's Prime Minister and then President after his country gained independence in 1963. 'Gentlemen of the Jungle' is included in his study of the Gikuyu, *Facing Mount Kenya* (1938), as a Gikuyu story which illustrates 'the relation between the Gikuyu and the Europeans'.

Leonard Kibera grew up during Kenya's Emergency. He has published a novel, *Voices in the Dark*, and (with his brother Samuel Kahiga) a collection of stories, *Potent Ash*.

Dambudzo Marechera (born 1955) grew up in Zimbabwe, was expelled from the University of Rhodesia and continued his studies at Oxford. He has published two works of fiction, *The House of Hunger*, a volume of short stories which was awarded *The Guardian* Fiction Prize and a novel, *Black Sunlight*.

Ezekiel Mphahlele (born 1919) recorded his boyhood in Pretoria in his autobiographical *Down Second Avenue*. He has published three collections of stories, *Man Must Live*, *The Living and the Dead*, and *In Corner B*, a novel, *The Wanderers*, and several works of criticism. After many years in exile in Nigeria, Kenya, France and the United States, Mphahlele has returned to South Africa.

Ngugi wa Thiong'o (born 1938) is East Africa's best known writer. His four novels in English, *The River Between*, *Weep Not Child*, *A Grain of Wheat* and *Petals of Blood*, and one in Gikuyu *Caitaani Mutharaba-ini* (translated as *Devil on the Cross*), record the struggle against colonial and neocolonial oppression in Kenya. He has also written plays, a volume of short stories, *Secret Lives*, and two volumes of critical essays. He was detained for a year in Kenya after the first performances of his Gikuyu drama, *Ngaahika Ndeenda* (1977), published in English as *I Will Marry When I Want*, and has lived in exile since the political imprisonment of many Kenyan lecturers and students in 1982.

Grace Ogot (born 1930) grew up in Kenya's Central Nyanza District, and has worked as a nurse and midwifery tutor, a scriptwriter and broadcaster, a Community Development Officer, and in Public Relations. She has published a novel, *The Promised Land*, and is well-known as a short story writer. Some of her stories are collected in *Land Without Thunder*.

Sembene Ousmane, film director and writer, was born in Senegal in 1923. He worked as a fisherman, plumber, bricklayer and mechanic before becoming a docker and trade union leader in Marseilles, and out of this experience he wrote *Le Docker Noir* (1956). His other novels and short stories include *Les Bouts de Bois de Dieu* (translated as *God's Bits of Wood*), *Voltaique* (*Tribal Scars*), *Le Mandat* (*The Money Order*), *Xala* and *Le Dernier de l'Empire* (*The Last of the Empire*). He has made several films including *Le Mandat* and *Xala*.

David Owoyele was a Yoruba from Northern Nigeria, where he worked as an officer in the Information Services. His short stories and articles have been published in a number of journals and anthologies.

Alifa Rifaat grew up in Egypt and now lives in Cairo. She has published two collections of short stories in Arabic, and recently her work has been translated into English by Denys Johnson-Davies and published under the title, *Distant View of a Minaret* (Quartet).

Tayeb Salih was born in the Northern Province of the Sudan in 1929 and grew up in a farming community. He was Head of Drama in the BBC's Arabic Service, and now works for UNESCO in Paris. A short novel and several stories are translated from Arabic and published under the title *The Wedding of Zein*.

Acknowledgements

The editors wish to thank Robyn Scofield for her help and advice in the preliminary selection of stories for this anthology.

The editors and publishers would like to thank the following for permission to reproduce copyright material:

African Universities Press, Ibadan for 'The Will of Allah' by David Owoyele.

Ama Ata Aidoo for 'Certain Wind from the South'.

Dr F. Odun Balogun for 'The Apprentice' by Odun Balogun originally published in *Okike* 14, 1978.

David Bolt Associates, London and Doubleday & Company, Inc., New York for 'Civil Peace' by Chinua Achebe, originally published in *Okike* 2, 1971.

East African Publishing House, Nairobi for 'The Green Leaves' by Grace Ogot from *Land Without Thunder*, 'The Spider's Web' by Leonard Kibera from *Potent Ash*, and 'The Coffee-Cart Girl' by Ezekiel Mphahlele from *In Corner B*.

Abdulrazak Gurnah for 'Bossy', originally published in *Okike* 13, 1978.

Heinemann Educational Books, London for 'A Handful of Dates' by Tayeb Salih from *The Wedding of Zein*, 'Protista' by Dambudzo Marechera from *The House of Hunger*, and 'Snapshots of a Wedding' by Bessie Head from *The Collector of Treasures*.

Heinemann Educational Books, London and Lawrence Hill & Co. Publishers Inc., Westport, Connecticut for 'Minutes of Glory' by Ngugi wa Thiong'o from *Secret Lives*.

Acknowledgements

Heinemann Educational Books, London and Three Continents Press, Washington D.C. for a 'Conversation from the Third Floor' by Mohamed El-Bisatie from *Egyptian Short Stories*.

Presence Africaine, Paris for 'The False Prophet' by Sembene Ousmane from *Tribal Scars*.

Quartet Books, London for 'An Incident in the Ghobashi Household' by Alifa Rifaat from *Distant View of a Minaret*.

Random House Inc., New York and Martin Secker & Warburg Ltd., London for 'Gentlemen of the Jungle' by Jomo Kenyatta from *Facing Mount Kenya*.

Ravan Press (Pty) Ltd., Johannesburg for 'The Betrayal' by Ahmed Essop from *The Haaji and Other Stories* and 'Reflections in a Cell' by Mafika Gwala from *Staffrider* (April/May, 1981).

A.P. Watt Ltd., London for 'Papa, Snake and I' by L.B Honwana (© Luis Bernado Honwana 1969), and 'The Bride-groom' by Nadine Gordimer from *Friday's Footprint*.

WEST AFRICA

The False Prophet

Sembene Ousmane

translated by Len Ortzen

Mahmoud Fall, with his bronze countenance, aquiline nose and his rapid walk—though not so rapid as the hawk-like glance of his eyes—came of a line of Senegalese Muslims, faithfully abiding by his ancestors' motto, 'What is mine belongs to me, but there is nothing to stop us sharing what is yours', he did no work. Or to be exact, he did not like killing himself with work. When children slyly asked him, 'Mahmoud, why aren't there any cats where you come from?' he would answer, 'I don't really know.'

It was his way of avoiding saying that cats, like him, liked to be fed without doing anything—which is why there are none to be seen in Upper Senegal. The land there is arid, and the inhabitants erect their tents at nightfall and strike them at dawn. An animal cannot live at man's expense when man is a nomad. Like clings to like, it is said. But these two shun each other. And any cat seen perchance in that country is a pitiful sight.

Mahmoud Fall, tired of doing nothing, with his pockets empty, had decided to journey towards the sunset and the country of the Bilals. In his view these ebony-skinned men were his inferiors, only good for guarding the harem, after having been castrated which eliminates disputes over the paternity of the children.

When he reached Senegal, Mahmoud Fall changed his name. He called himself Aidra, a name which opened all doors to him. He was received everywhere with the respect due to his rank. Having studied the Koran in Mauretania—something that the Senegalese always regard with respect—he profited from his knowledge of the Holy Book, presiding over prayers and sinking into interminable genuflexions. The local

people were awestruck; they considered it a very great honour
to have a descendant of the noble Aidra as their Imam.

Like his counterpart the cat, Mahmoud arched his back
under all these praises. As nature had endowed him with a
fine singing voice he was able to delight those around him,
making every effort to modulate the syllables before flattening
them at the end of each verse. He spent the time between each
of the five daily prayers squatting on a sheepskin and telling
his beads.

When mealtime came, Mahmoud insisted upon being
served apart from the others. The only thanks he gave was to
sprinkle children and adults with his abundant spittle. They all
rubbed this over their faces, saying 'Amen, amen'. One won-
ders what Mahmoud thought of all this in the secrecy of his
conscience and when he was alone with God.

Being used to moving around, he went from compound to
compound and was always received according to the traditional code: 'To each stranger his bowl.' The guest did not refuse
anything at first, but as the days went by he became more and
more fastidious. According to him, couscous prevented him
from sleeping and he complained of indigestion. As his hosts
were anxious to remain on the path which leads to Paradise,
they cooked special dishes likely to appeal to such a discerning
palate as his. But to make certain he did not hesitate at times to
go into the kitchen to order what he fancied. That was the
brotherly aspect.

Besides being well fed, Mahmoud Fall was amassing small
coins, though he never considered there were enough of them
for the trouble he was taking. These blacks definitely had a low
regard for the value of prayer. And there was another thing—
why did they persist in keeping cats? Each time he saw one in a
house he felt his hair stand on end, just like the fur of an angry
tom-cat. He pulled a face and chased the cat out. Sometimes he
preached on the uselessness of cats.

Despite these trifling annoyances, Mahmoud Fall felt that
over the months his reputation as a preacher was growing.
Learned and holy men everywhere, the talebs, marabouts and
tafsirs, had but one phrase on their lips: '*Souma Narr, Souma
Narr* (My Moor, My Moor).' Mahmoud secretly thought they
were mad. '*Souma Narr*! My Moor. Why *my*? Has anyone ever

heard of a black buying a Moor? That would be a topsy-turvy kind of world!'

He wrote more and more signs on pieces of paper for people to carry around with them, and he worked harder than ever to hide his origins and his real aim. To increase his prestige even more, he went so far as to declare that his body was banished from Finahri Dianan—from Hell. And they swallowed that with all the rest.

As the months passed, Mahmoud saw that his hoard was steadily increasing. And one morning, without a word to anyone, he departed as unexpectedly as he had arrived one evening. The elders in their wisdom said, 'If the setting sun brings a stranger, don't look for him at sunrise.'

* * * * *

With his booty in a bag slung over his shoulder, Mahmoud Fall headed briskly towards his beloved Atlas mountains. He walked day and night, with only short rests, thinking of how he would use his capital and taking care to avoid any doubtful encounters. To this end, he made a detour towards the north, which took him through the kingdom of the Tiedes, heathens who worshipped fetishes—though Mahmoud was unaware of this. As he went, he kept congratulating himself: 'Thanks to Satan, I have a great knowledge of the art of appropriating other people's possessions.'

It was the height of the dry season. The sun's rays, like flamethrowers, were setting fire to the sparse tufts of grass; the wind tore at them and flung them towards the far-distant shores, whistling as though to put an end to the unendurable monotony of silence. From the overheated earth there issued a vapour rising to the empty sky. There were the carcasses of animals which had been picked clean at every stage of decomposition and which the wind was gradually burying in the sand. The birds of the air passing uttered cries which were like complaints made to nature. A blend of serenity and unease.

As far as Mahmoud could see, there was no sign of any living being. Only a single tree. A strange tree—strange because of its abundant foliage. The sole survivor in that hell. A tamarind tree.

It was almost the time for prayer. Tired out from his long

trek and overcome by the heat, Mahmoud lingered by the tree, wondering whether to pray before or after sleeping. He had to make a decision, and finally he opted for sleep and lay down under the tamarind tree. But what was this? Suddenly he sat up and gave a shout, very loud, although he was alone. 'Hey! Hey! Yes, you up there, come down!'

His words echoed around. Three times he called out, but no reply came. Then he got up, ran to the right and the left, towards the setting sun and to the east. But he was quite alone. There was just him and the tree. An inner voice, doubly suspicious, urged him to bury his treasure. He dug down the length of his forearm; then went to investigate the surroundings, but found nothing. He returned and dug twice as deep, went off again; still nothing. No one at all. He shielded his eyes to peer more clearly into the tree's thick foliage. No one was hiding there. Then he went back to his hole and dug still deeper. This done, he sat down in it and counted his *derhems* which chinked agreeably in the silence. Pleased and reassured, he buried them all, then stretched out to sleep on top of his hoard. But he remembered that he had not paid his due to the Almighty, and addressed Him thus: 'I owe it to you. . .'

After all this performance, sleep was not long in coming to Mahmoud. It was accompanied by a sweet dream in which he was drifting through the desert. As far as the eye could see stretched a vast ocean of sand with interweaving slopes of the dunes. Like ships of this silent sea, camels were plodding along, heads nodding on their long necks; despite the storm that was blowing, the reins were held in position by their brass nose-rings. Grains of sand, harder than steel, pricked through his clothes and stung the skin. Then the dream changed into some sort of reality. Mahmoud Fall saw himself lifted up by a very thin, half-naked black. The man ransacked his hoard, then deliberately proceeded to shave his head. Mahmoud eventually roused himself, still dazed with sleep, thanked God and yawned.

As a good believer, Mahmoud thought of the first prayer of the day. (If no water is available, sand ablutions are allowed.) He first trickled some sand over his hands and arms to cleanse them of everything unclean he had touched, then sprinkled some over his face and head. In carrying out this ritual he had a

shock—he had not felt his mane of hair. He hurriedly put both
hands to his head, fingering it all over. He had no hair—his
head was bald. Slowly, carefully, making a great effort to
control himself, Mahmoud drew his hands down to his chin.
His beard had gone too. Wild-eyed and aghast, Mahmoud
became aware of something strange happening within him.
He thought he could hear voices. And this was so, but they
were inner voices.

'It was God who shaved you,' said the first.

'How do you make that out? God doesn't shave anyone.'

Mahmoud, listening to this dialogue, grew livid. The next
comment was greeted with a laugh.

'Have faith in God, His mercy is in everything!'

'Ha, ha! You make me laugh. And when you fleeced those
poor blighters, in whose name did you do it?'

Mahmoud vigorously shook his head to try to silence these
voices, but to no effect; so he put his hands over his ears. He
did not want to hear any more. But the voices continued:

'Pray!' one commanded him. 'You have missed two prayers
already.'

'Look for your money first,' advised the other. 'Without it,
you won't be respected. You won't have any camels. You'll
have nothing to eat. Make sure of your money first. It's easier
to pray when you're sure of having a full belly.'

Mahmoud obeyed the last injunction. He scrabbled around,
casting earth and sand aside so vigorously that his actions
were quite unlike those of a normal human being. A goat at
bay bites; and Mahmoud would have bitten anyone who tried
to stop him looking for his hoard. He was sweating as he
crouched there with his tongue hanging out. He could easily
have been taken for a giant crab. He pushed the earth away
from the hole with his feet. His enveloping *boubou* was half-
strangling him, so he wrenched the neck open and then dug
down with renewed energy. At last he reached the bottom,
and there to his dismay all he found was his sleek, black hair.

He lifted it up, glanced at it in bewilderment, then stared
down at the empty hole. Raising his eyes to the tree, he took
God as his witness, '*Bilahi-vahali*, this isn't me.'

As he held his hair in one hand and stroked his shaved head
with the other, tears welled up in his eyes, '*Bilahi-vahali*, I'm

not Mahmoud Fall!' he said again, a sob in his voice.

Then he shouted at the top of his voice, 'My friend, my old friend Mahmoud Fall, come and deliver me from this uncertainty!'

The echo whisked away his call, rolling it over before hurling it on to the plain like a stone on to a galvanized-iron roof. The sound faded into the distance, and he murmured slowly, 'My old friend Mahmoud Fall, don't play this trick on me. I've known you for a long time. . .'

He strained his ears, listening hard, concentrating on a point beyond his range of vision; but he heard nothing. Just a vast emptiness. Then the mocking voices returned.

'Aren't you going to pray?' said the first.

Hardly aware of what he was doing, he stood up, faced towards Mecca, and raised his hands to his temples, '*Allah ackbar!* God is great,' he began.

But his eyes wandered to where his hoard had been hidden.

'Can you still pray when you've been robbed?'

'Ask God who the thief is,' said the other voice.

Mahmoud stood there with his arms raised, not knowing what to do. Then he remembered his dream. 'I wasn't asleep,' he thought.

He had seen the thief; he had even felt that he was being shorn. And the Almighty had not intervened, the Almighty had let it be done.

'No, I'm not going to pray any more,' he said in a low voice, thinking that Allah would not hear him.

Three times he walked round the tree, hoping to find footprints; but in vain. High in the sky, a migrating bird began to sing cheerfully. Mahmoud Fall shouted curses at it. Then he suddenly felt himself to be very much alone.

'On the word of a Moor,' he murmured, 'these sons of slaves are all thieves!'

Rage possessed him, and he ran off like a madman into the desert, his torn *boubou* flapping in the wind. He had just realized that there is no need to believe in Allah in order to be a thief!

Certain Winds from the South

Ama Ata Aidoo

M'ma Asana eyed the wretched pile of cola-nuts, spat, and picked up the reed-bowl. Then she put down the bowl, picked up one of the nuts, bit at it, threw it back, spat again, and stood up. First, a sharp little ache, just a sharp little one, shot up from somewhere under her left ear. Then her eyes became misty.

'I must check on those logs,' she thought, thinking this misting of her eyes was due to the chill in the air. She stooped over the nuts.

'You never know what evil eyes are prowling this dust over these grasslands, I must pick them up quickly.'

On the way back to the kraal her eyes fell on the especially patchy circles that marked where the old pits had been. At this time, in the old days, they would have been nearly bursting and as one scratched out the remains of the out-going season, one felt a near-sexual thrill of pleasure looking at these pits, just as one imagines a man might feel who looks upon his wife in the ninth month of pregnancy.

Pregnancy and birth and death and pain; and death again . . . when there are no more pregnancies, there are no more births, and therefore, no more deaths. But there is only one death and only one pain.

Show me a fresh corpse, my sister, so I can weep you old tears.

The pit of her belly went cold, then her womb moved and she had to lean by the doorway. In twenty years Fuseni's has been the only pregnancy and the only birth. Twenty years, and the first child and a male! In the old days, there would have been bucks and you got scolded for serving a woman in maternity a duicker. But these days those mean poachers on the government reserves sneak away their miserable duickers, such wretched hinds! Yes they sneak away even the duickers to the houses of those sweet-toothed southerners.

In the old days, how time goes, and how quickly age comes. But then does one expect to grow younger when one starts getting grandchildren? Allah be praised for a grandson.

The fire was still strong when she returned to the room. M'ma Asana put the nuts down. She craned her neck into the corner. At least those logs should take them to the following week. For the rest of the evening, she sat about preparing for the morrow's marketing.

The evening prayers were done. The money was in the bag. The grassland was still, Hawa was sleeping and so was Fuseni. M'ma came out to the main gate, first to check up if all was well outside and then to draw the door across. It was not the figure, but rather the soft rustle of light footsteps trying to move still more lightly over the grass, that caught her attention.

'If only it could be my husband.'

But of course it was not her husband!

'Who comes?'

'It is me, M'ma.'

'You, Issa, my son?'

'Yes, M'ma.'

'They are asleep.'

'I thought so. That is why I am coming now.'

There was a long pause in the conversation as they both hesitated about whether the son-in-law should go in to see Hawa and the baby or not. Nothing was said about this struggle but then one does not say everything.

M'ma Asana did not see but felt him win the battle. She crossed the threshold outside and drew the door behind her. Issa led the way. They did not walk far, however. They just turned into a corner between two of the projecting pillars in the wall of the kraal. It was as it should have been for it was he who needed the comforting coolness of it for his backbone.

'M'ma, is Fuseni well?'

'Yes.'

'M'ma, is Hawa well?'

'Yes.'

'M'ma please tell me, is Fuseni very well?'

'A-ah, my son. For what are you troubling yourself so much? Fuseni is a new baby who was born not more than ten days ago. How can I tell you he is very well? When a grown-up goes to live in other people's village. . .'

'M'ma?'

'What is it?'

'No. Please, it is nothing.'

'My son, I cannot understand you this evening . . . yes, if you, a grown-up person, go to live in another village, will you say after the first few days that you are perfectly well?'

'No.'

'Shall you not get yourself used to their food? Shall you not find first where you can get water for yourself and your sheep?'

'Yes, M'ma.'

'Then how is it you ask me if Fuseni is very well? The navel is healing very fast . . . and how would it not? Not a single navel of all that I have cut here got infected. Shall I now cut my grandson's and then sit and see it rot? But it is his male that I can't say. Mallam did it neat and proper and it must be all right. Your family is not noted for males that rot, is it now?'

'No, M'ma,'

'Then let your heart lie quiet in your breast. Fuseni is well but we cannot say how well yet.'

'I have heard you, M'ma. M'ma?'

'Yes, my son.'

'M'ma, I am going south.'

'Where did you say?'

'South.'

'How far?'

'As far as the sea. M'ma, I thought you would understand.'

'Have I spoken yet?'

'No, you have not.'

'Then why did you say that?'

'That was not well said.'

'And what are you going to do there?'

'Find some work.'

'What work?'

'I do not know.'

'Yes, you know, you are going to cut grass.'

'Perhaps.'

'But my son, why must you travel that far just to cut grass? Is there not enough of it all round here? Around this kraal, your father's and all the others in the village? Why do you not cut these?'

'M'ma, you know it is not the same. If I did that here people would think I was mad. But over there, I have heard that not only do they like it but the government pays you to do it.'

'Even so, our men do not go south to cut grass. This is for those further north. They of the wilderness, it is they who go south to cut grass. This is not for our men.'

'Please M'ma, already time is going. Hawa is a new mother and Fuseni my first child.'

'And yet you are leaving them to go south and cut grass.'

'But M'ma, what will be the use of my staying here and watching them starve? You yourself know that all the cola went bad, and even if they had not, with trade as it is, how much money do you think I would have got from them? And that is why I am going. Trade is broken and since we do not know when things will be good again, I think it will be better for me to go away.'

'Does Hawa know?'

'No, she does not.'

'Are you coming to wake her up at this late hour to tell her?'

'No.'

'You are wise.'

'M'ma, I have left everything in the hands of Amadu. He will come and see Hawa tomorrow.'

'Good.'

'When shall we expect you back?'

'Issa.'

'M'ma.'

'When shall we expect you back?'

'M'ma, I do not know. Perhaps next Ramadan.'

'Good.'

'So I go now.'

'Allah go with you.'

'And may His prophet look after you all.'

M'ma went straight back to bed, but not to sleep. And how could she sleep? At dawn, her eyes were still wide open.

'Is his family noted for males that rot? No, certainly not. It is us who are noted for our unlucky females. There must be

something wrong with them . . . Or how is it we cannot hold
our men? Allah, how is it?

'Twenty years ago. Twenty years, perhaps more than twenty years . . . perhaps more than twenty years and Allah,
please, give me strength to tell Hawa.

'Or shall I go to the market now and then tell her when I
come back? No. Hawa, Hawa, now look at how you are
stretched down there like a log! Does a mother sleep like this?
Hawa, H-a-a-w-a! Oh, I shall not leave you alone . . . and how
can you hear your baby when it cries in the night since you die
when you sleep?

'Listen to her asking me questions! Yes, it is broad daylight. I
thought you really were dead. If it is cold, draw your blanket
round you and listen to me for I have something to tell you.

'Hawa, Issa has gone south.

'And why do you stare at me with such shining eyes. I am
telling you that Issa is gone south.

'And what question do you think you are asking me? How
could he take you along when you have a baby whose navel
wound has not even healed yet?

'He went away last night.

'Don't ask me why I did not come and wake you up. What
should I have woken you up for? Listen, Issa said he could not
stay here and just watch you and Fuseni starve.

'He is going south to find work, and . . . Hawa, where do
you think you are getting up to go? Issa is not at the door
waiting for you. The whole neighbourhood is not up yet, so do
not let me shout . . . and why are you behaving like a baby?
Now you are a mother and you must decide to grow up . . .
where are you getting up to go? Listen to me telling you this.
Issa is gone. He went last night because he wants to catch the
government bus that leaves Tamale very early in the morning.
So . . .

'Hawa, ah-ah, are you crying? Why are you crying? That
your husband has left you to go and work? Go on weeping, for
he will bring the money to look after me and not you . . .

'I do not understand, you say? Maybe I do not . . . See, now
you have woken up Fuseni. Sit down and feed him and listen
to me.

'Listen to me and I will tell you of another man who left his newborn child and went away.

'Did he come back? No, he did not come back. But do not ask me any more questions for I will tell you all.

'He used to go and come, then one day he went away and never came back. Not that he had to go like the rest of them. . .

'Oh, they were soldiers. I am talking of a soldier. He need not have gone to be a soldier. After all, his father was one of the richest men of this land. He was not the eldest son, that is true, but still there were so many things he could have done to look after himself and his wife when he came to marry. But he would not listen to anybody. How could he sit by and have other boys out-do him in smartness?

'Their clothes that shone and shone with pressing . . . I say, you could have looked into any of them and put khole under your eyes. And their shoes, how they roared! You know soldiers for yourself. Oh, the stir on the land when they came in from the south! Mothers spoke hard and long to daughters about the excellencies of proper marriages, while fathers hurried through with betrothals. Most of them were afraid of getting a case like that of Memunat on their hands. Her father had taken the cattle and everything and then Memunat goes and plays with a soldier. Oh, the scandal she caused herself then!

'Who was this Memunat? No, she is not your friend's mother. No, this Memunat in the end ran away south herself. We hear she became a bad woman in the city and made a lot of money.

'No, we do not hear of her now. She is not dead either, for we hear such women usually go to their homes to die, and she has not come back here yet.

'But us, we are different. I had not been betrothed.

'Do you ask me why I say "we"? Because this man was your father. Ah-ah, you open your mouth and eyes wide? Yes, my child, it is of your father I am speaking.

'No, I was not lying when I told you that he died. But keep quiet and listen. He was going south to get himself a house for married soldiers.

'No, it was not that time he did not come back. He came here, but not to fetch me.

'He asked us if we had heard of the war.

'Had we not heard of the war? Was it not difficult to get things like tinned fish, kerosene and cloth?

'Yes, we said, but we thought it was only because the traders were not bringing them in.

'Well yes, he said, but the traders do not get them even in the south.

'And why, we asked.

'Oh you people, have you not heard of the German people? He had no patience with us. He told us that in the south they were singing dirty songs with their name.

'But when are we going, I asked him?

'What he told me was that that was why he had come. He could not take me along with him. You see, he said we were under the Anglis-people's rule and they were fighting with the German-people.

'Ask me, my child, for that was exactly what I asked him. What has all that got to do with you and me? Why can I not come south with you?'

'Because I have to travel to the lands beyond the sea and fight.

'In other people's war? My child, it is as if you were there, that is what I asked him.

'But it is not as simple as that, he said.

'We could not understand him. You shall not go, said his father. You shall not go, for it is not us fighting with the Grunshies or the Gonjas.

'I know about the Anglis-people but not about any German-people, but anyway they are in their country.

'Of course his father was playing, and so was I.

'A soldier must obey at all times, he said.

'I wanted to give him so many things to take with him but he said he could only take cola.

'Then the news came. It did not enter my head, for it was all empty. Everything went into my womb. You were just three days old.

'The news was like fire which settled in the pit of my belly. And from time to time, some will shoot up, searing my womb, singeing my intestines and burning up and up and up until I screamed with madness when it got into my head.

'I had told myself when you were born that it did not matter you were a girl. All gifts from Allah are good and anyway he was coming back and we were going to have many more children, lots of sons.

'But Hawa, you had a lot of strength, for how you managed to live I do not know. Three days you were and suddenly like a rivulet that is hit by an early harmattan, my breasts went dry. Hawa, you have a lot of strength.

'Later, they told me that if I could go south and prove to the government's people that I was his wife I would get a lot of money.

'But I did not go. It was him I wanted not his body turned into gold.

'I never saw the south.

'Do you say "oh"? My child I am always telling you that the world was created a long while ago and it is old-age one has seen but not youth. So do not say "oh".

'Those people, the government's people, who come and go, tell us trade is bad now, and once again there is no tinned fish and no cloth. But this time they say this is because our children are going to get them in abundance one day.

'Issa has gone south now because he cannot afford even goat flesh for his wife in maternity. This has to be, so that Fuseni can stay with his wife and eat cow-meat with her? Hmm. And he will come back alive . . . perhaps not next Ramadan but the next. Now my daughter, you know of another man who went to fight. And he went to fight in other people's war and he never came back.

'I am going to the market now. Get up early to wash Fuseni. I hope to get something for those miserable colas. There is enough rice for two, is there not?

'Good. Today even if it takes all the money, I hope to get us some smoked fish, the biggest I can find, to make us a real good sauce.'

The Apprentice

Odun Balogun

Ogunmola survived the ordeal of his apprenticeship thanks to his having a past. A past that traced back to Oba. Oba, his great grandfather. Oba, the illustrious. The wise ruler.

Ogunmola had the choice of going to school, but he would not. He had witnessed the fate of his grandfather and this had decided his position once and for all.

He was a mere child at the time. His grandfather was at the height of his glorious rule. Life was moving on meaningfully. Just as it had during the reign of the illustrious Oba, his father. He enjoyed the love and respect of his subjects. Peace and quiet dominated. Contentedness and accord prevailed. . .

Then suddenly they came. Uninvited. As if that was not enough, they said his grandfather did not know how to rule. His grandfather! The offspring of the illustrious Oba! One whose ability to rule in the times of poverty and riches, sedition and peace, pestilence and health had become a legend!

And that was not all. Life, they claimed, was being led not altogether the way it should. Everything had to be overhauled. A new beginning was necessary. . .

And indeed they immediately started to effect the changes. With inhuman speed and haste. Ogunmola, a mere child, saw it all. He was confused by it. But he had no difficulty in understanding the cause of the premature death of his grandfather. He was horrified to realise that his father could not become king after his grandfather. No one would continue the rule of Oba, his illustrious great grandfather! He himself could have no pretentions. . .

In spite of this they wanted him to go to school! To put his stamp on those changes and proclaim them God-sent and just! Him, Ogunmola, the great grandchild of Oba, the wise ruler!

Never. Never, never, never. His royal blood revolted vehemently against the suggestion to succumb to an inglorious domination, to the worship of a false god. And he was a mere child.

But he had to do something. He had been born. What did it matter that the times were like this? Was that not the purpose of his birth? To make meaning of a life like this?

Ogunmola took up the challenge. He decided to become a master blacksmith. His years of apprenticeship began. Life was going to be meaningful from now on. So he thought.

He was mistaken. It was only then that his troubles actually began. It was hardly a year since he had been with Omotaiye, his master, when the latter called him aside:

'Ogunmola', he began in his gentle, humane voice, 'you know I love you like a son, and that I have the highest respect for you as an apprentice. I believe you will make my name great yet. And that is why I'm grieved at what I see in your works lately.'

Ogunmola loved and respected his master. So it was with deep concern he heard these words. Emotions choked his voice as he said:

'May I know what grieves you, master? If it is within my power I will do everything to alleviate it.'

'When I look at the hoes, cutlasses, knives and other implements you forge,' the master continued, 'they show no definite character, they are amorphous. However minutely I scrutinise them, they fail to reflect the lessons I have been at pains to teach you. I have repeatedly said that your aim should be to forge a hoe that is both practical and cheap. What's the use of a beautiful hoe if everybody, *everybody* cannot afford it? As things are going now, people will soon begin to say that you are the apprentice of Omotola.' Thus concluded the master in a tone of the deepest regret.

For Omotaiye to say that the work of his apprentice resembled that from Omotola's workshop was the most serious criticism that Omotaiye could ever make against anyone that studied under him. Ogunmola knew this and was troubled. He agreed essentially with his master, but he felt within himself the existence of something. Something exclusively his own which he could bring to the forging of a hoe that would make that hoe more practical, more cheap, more attainable and more beautiful. For this reason he experimented endlessly. Little by little he approached his goal. But the closer he got to this goal, the more the hoes he forged differed from those of his master. He had noticed this and was worried, but he had hoped that his master would not perceive the difference. But alas. . .

'Master', Ogunmola began excusing himself, 'you know I'm not imitating Omotola. I'm only trying to forge hoes my own way.'

'You're talking nonsense, my boy. That's an old story. It's all they say when they are actually turning against you. But for you to do that! You, whom I love so! You, who is . . .' The master was overpowered with emotions and could not continue. In a moment, however, he straightened up and added in a stern, uncompromising voice: 'Remember, if you choose to be my enemy, don't forget: an enemy is an enemy.'

Ogunmola was frightened, but he managed to say:

'I'm not your enemy, master.'

He was not believed. Life subsequently became difficult for him in his master's workshop. He tried to kill his initiative. All the same anything he forged bore a quality that was not his master's. Something unmistakably his own. In the eyes of his master, however, this something showed increasing resemblance to products from Omotola's workshop. His love for his apprentice changed into dislike, and soon it matured into enmity. Explanations didn't help. They only made things worse.

During this trying period Ogunmola sought to survive the cruel reality of his apprenticeship by escaping into his past. He recollected the stories of his illustrious family as they were narrated to him by his mother. It was as if he had witnessed the events with his own eyes. Every night be dreamt of Oba, his great grandfather, the wise ruler. He thrilled with joy in his sleep as he relived the last heroic deed of Oba.

'The plague came suddenly,' his mother had told him. 'Oba was ruling at the time. There was plenty. People were contented. Life was simple and meaningful. Then suddenly the plague!

'The effects were swift and disastrous. People died in hundreds. Soon it became evident that the population would be wiped out. It was then the wise men consulted the oracles.

'The Spirit of the land had been offended. An unusual atonement demanded. A man must sacrifice himself in expiation. No influence exerted. The choice completely voluntary. Sole motivation—the individual's love for the people. Otherwise the Spirit would not be appeased.' Thus spoke all the oracles.

'For a long time nobody volunteered. People began dying in thousands. It was then, early one morning, that Oba, the wise ruler, the beloved of his subjects, called his family together. He hugged everyone with tender emotions and then announced his intentions.

'Words spread like a wild fire. Dissuasions increased every second. The population consulted together and sent a delegation. "It is not enough that we should die like chickens? Must we also be left without a ruler? And a ruler like you? We would all die rather than lose you." These and many more were the words spoken. But Oba would not be dissuaded.

'It was a gloomy afternoon. Sorrow was in every heart. Fear written on every face. Oba, the illustrious, the wise ruler, walked calmly towards the Hill. Absolute silence reigned in the crowd of grieving subjects escorting their beloved ruler on his last journey. The gloomy silence was frequently pierced by heart-rending wailings that gushed forth from the desolate houses on the route. The bereaved mourned their dead. Almost at every step someone from the procession, who only a moment ago had been most actively alive, would suddenly stiffen and drop stone dead. Like a rotten dry wood blown down by the wind. Sorrow in every heart. Fear on every face.

'Oba hastened his steps. Soon he was at the edge of the precipice. Unspeakable fear gripped everyone as the wise ruler jumped the Hill. He vanished without a trace into the bottomless abyss.

'The Spirit of the land was pacified. A new life began. Your grandfather assumed the throne. He followed in the footsteps of Oba, his illustrious father, your great grandfather, the pride of the land. Once again the land knew splendour, subjects enjoyed plenty and comfort, life was simple and meaningful . . .

'And suddenly they came. Uninvited . . . You know the rest of the story, my son.' Thus concluded his mother. Her voice sad.

His mother had died seven years ago, but the recollection of this story made him feel as if she was once again alive; as if he himself was once more a six-year-old carefree child. He was happy, relieved by the knowledge that life had once been meaningful, that once there had been a king who knew how to rule, that one day there might yet be another. . .

These thoughts were Ogunmola's succour in the trying days of his apprenticeship. Omotaiye soon got to hate him bitterly, and before long the master asked his apprentice to leave. Without a certificate testifying to the completion of his apprenticeship, Ogunmola could not practise. This even though he felt he had acquired enough of the basics on which he could build to become a great master himself. Thus he found himself on the other side of the river, knocking on Omotola's door.

'Eh, see who is here! Come in. Come right in. Haven't I always said you're welcome in my house? Yes . . . really! I'm not actually surprised. Isn't it common knowledge that Omotaiye is mad? I'm happy it happened, though. I have always dreamt of having an apprentice like you. With me it will be completely different. You'll be free to forge any kinds of hoes, cutlasses, knives and other implements exactly the way you like. Absolutely free. Of course, who would think of forging a hoe that is not durable as well as being beautiful? People know they are buying quality and, naturally, they're prepared to pay something extra. Why worry about every Tom, Dick and Harry? Where is the guarantee that even if their Dick could afford our hoe that he'll make good use of it? So, you see, you're welcome. Come right in.'

This was how Ogunmola was received by Omotola, the arch enemy of Omotaiye, his former master. Ogunmola understood the condition of his acceptance, but he also knew that he had been promised freedom. However, a year had hardly gone by when Omotola called him for an explanation.

'I have given you sufficient time to get rid of all that non-sense with which Omotaiye had stuffed your head. Apparently, you're not in a hurry. Perhaps you don't even intend to . . . Yes, yes, I quite understand. Far more than you suppose. You

all say that even at the very moment you're going against one.
But it's an old game, my boy, and the answer is as old as the
Bible. You cannot serve two masters. So you're either for me or
against me. And it's time you declared your stand.'

Again life became bitter for Ogunmola. What was he to do?
He had sought to safeguard his honour by refusing to go to
school but had ended up making things more difficult. And all
because in this cruel time it was enough to be caught in the
family quarrels of strangers to be denied one's dignity, one's
rights.

Omotaiye and Omotola, as rumour had it, were twins.
Identical twins. One was as tall and athletic as the other, as
healthy and boisterous as the other, as courageous and ambi-
tious as the other, as talented and hard-working as the other,
as tempered and diplomatic as the other, as good a master as
the other, as . . .

One could go on for ever enumerating the points of similar-
ity. Yet these twins would be the very first to deny the
existence of any such similarities, of any kind of relationship.
They had never known each other from Adam. Didn't you
study Geography? How could you possibly confuse someone who lives on this side of the river with the one on the
other side? Can't you recognise the signs of the time? Then,
why won't you differentiate between the road that leads forward into the future from the one that goes backward into the
past . . .?

The arguments were inexhaustible.

Ogunmola heard it all and was at a loss to explain that it was
his least desire to serve as an arbiter in a family quarrel, that he
did not want to be caught in the crossfire between two
brothers, that his sole desire was to be a smith; a simple smith,
forging hoes his own way and dreaming of Oba, the wise
ruler, his grandfather when the going was tough.

Was that asking too much? Ogunmola could not tell. He
knew only that this was a trying time and he wished he would
survive it.

The Will of Allah

David Owoyele

There had been a clear moon. Now the night was dark. Dogo glanced up at the night sky. He saw that scudding black clouds had obscured the moon. He cleared his throat. 'Rain tonight,' he observed to his companion. Sule, his companion, did not reply immediately. He was a tall powerfully-built man. His face, as well as his companion's, was a stupid mask of ignorance. He lived by thieving as did Dogo, and just now he walked with an unaccustomed limp. 'It is wrong to say that,' Sule said after a while, fingering the long, curved sheath-knife he always wore on his upper left arm when, in his own words, he was 'on duty'. A similar cruel-looking object adorned the arm of his comrade. 'How can you be sure?' 'Sure?' said Dogo, annoyance and impatience in his voice. Dogo is the local word for tall. This man was thickset, short and squat, anything but tall. He pointed one hand up at the scurrying clouds. 'You only want to look up there. A lot of rain has fallen in my life: those up there are rain clouds.'

They walked on in silence for a while. The dull red lights of the big town glowed in crooked lines behind them. Few people were abroad, for it was already past midnight. About half a mile ahead of them the native town, their destination, sprawled in the night. Not a single electric light bulb glowed on its crooked streets. This regrettable fact suited the books of the two men perfectly. 'You are not Allah,' said Sule at last. 'You may not assert.'

Sule was a hardened criminal. Crime was his livelihood, he had told the judge this during his last trial that had earned him a short stretch in jail. 'Society must be protected from characters like you,' he could still hear the stern judge intoning in the hushed courtroom. Sule had stood in the dock, erect, unashamed, unimpressed; he'd heard it all before. 'You and your type constitute a threat to life and property and this court will always see to it that you get your just deserts, according to the Law.' The judge had then fixed him with a stern gaze, which Sule coolly returned: he had stared into too many so-called judges' eyes to be easily intimidated. Besides, he feared nothing and no one except Allah. The judge thrust his legal chin forward. 'Do you never pause to consider that the road of crime leads only to frustration, punishment and suffering? You look fit enough for anything. Why don't you try your hand at earning an honest living for a change?' Sule had shrugged his broad shoulders. 'I earn my living the only way I know,' he said. 'The only way I've chosen.' The judge had sat back, dismayed. Then he leaned forward to try again. 'Is it beyond you to see anything wrong in thieving, burglary, crime?' Again Sule had shrugged. 'The way I earn my living I find quite satisfactory.' 'Satisfactory!' exclaimed the judge, and a wave of whispering swept over the court. The judge stopped this with a rap of his gavel. 'Do you find it satisfactory to break the law?' 'I've no choice,' said Sule. 'The law is a nuisance. It keeps getting in one's way.' 'Constant arrest and imprisonment—do you find it satisfactory to be a jailbird?' queried the judge, frowning most severely. 'Every calling has its hazards,' replied Sule philosophically. The judge mopped his face. 'Well, my man, you cannot break the law. You can only attempt to break it. And you will only end up by getting broken.' Sule nodded. 'We have a saying like that,' he remarked conversationally. 'He who attempts to shake a stump only shakes himself.' He glanced up at the frowning judge. 'Something like a thick stump—the law, eh?' The judge had given him three months. Sule had shrugged. 'The will of Allah be done. . .'

A darting tongue of lightning lit up the overcast sky for a second. Sule glanced up. 'Sure it looks like rain. But you do not say: It will rain. You are only a mortal. You only say: If it is the will of Allah, it will rain.' Sule was a deeply religious man, according to his lights. His religion forbade being dogmatic or prophetic about the future, about anything. His fear of Allah was quite genuine. It was his firm conviction that Allah left the question of a means of livelihood for each man to decide for himself. Allah, he was sure, gives some people more than they need so that others with too little could help themselves to

some of it. It could certainly not be the intention of Allah that
some stomachs remain empty while others are overstuffed.

Dogo snorted. He had served prison sentences in all the
major towns in the country. Prison had become for him a home
from home. Like his companion in crime, he feared no man;
but unlike him, he had no religion other than self-
preservation. 'You and your religion,' he said in derision. 'A
lot of good it has done you.' Sule did not reply. Dogo knew
from experience that Sule was touchy about his religion, and
the first intimation he would get that Sule had lost his temper
would be a blow on the head. The two men never pretended
that their partnership had anything to do with love or
friendship or any other luxurious idea: they operated together
when their prison sentences allowed because they found it
convenient. In a partnership that each believed was for his
own special benefit, there could be no fancy code of conduct.
'Did you see the woman tonight?' Dogo asked, changing the
subject, not because he was afraid of Sule's displeasure but
because his grasshopper mind had switched to something
else. 'Uh-huh,' granted Sule. 'Well?' said Dogo when he did
not go on. 'Bastard!' said Sule, without any passion. 'Who?
Me?' said Dogo thinly. 'We were talking about the woman,'
replied Sule.

They got to a small stream. Sule stopped, washed his arms
and legs, his clean-shaven head. Dogo squatted on the bank,
sharpening his sheath-knife on a stone. 'Where do you think
you are going?' 'To yonder village,' said Sule, rinsing out his
mouth. 'Didn't know you had a sweetheart there,' said Dogo.
'I'm not going to any woman,' said Sule. 'I am going to collect
stray odds and ends—if it is the will of Allah.'

'To steal, you mean?' suggested Dogo.

'Yes,' conceded Sule. He straightened himself, pointed a
brawny arm at Dogo: 'You are a burglar, too . . . and a bastard
besides.'

Dogo, calmly testing the edge of the knife on his arm,
nodded. 'Is that part of your religion, washing in midnight
streams?' Sule didn't reply until he had climbed on to the
farther bank, 'Wash when you find a stream; for when you
cross another is entirely in the hands of Allah.' He limped off,
Dogo following him. 'Why did you call her a bastard?' Dogo

asked. 'Because she is one.' 'Why?' 'She told me she sold the coat and the black bag for only fifteen shillings.' He glanced down and sideways at his companion. 'I suppose you got on to her before I did and told her what to say?' 'I've not laid eyes on her for a week,' protested Dogo. 'The coat is fairly old. Fifteen shillings sounds all right to me. I think she has done very well indeed.' 'No doubt,' said Sule. He didn't believe Dogo. 'I'd think the same way if I'd already shared part of the proceeds with her . . .'

Dogo said nothing. Sule was always suspicious of him, and he returned the compliment willingly. Sometimes their suspicion of each other was groundless, other times not. Dogo shrugged. 'I don't know what you are talking about.' 'No. I don't suppose you would,' said Sule drily. 'All I'm interested in is my share,' went on Dogo. 'Your second share, you mean,' said Sule. 'You'll both get your share—you cheating son without a father, as well as that howling devil of a woman.' He paused before he added, 'She stabbed me in the thigh—the bitch.' Dogo chuckled softly to himself. 'I've been wondering about that limp of yours. Put a knife in your thigh, did she? Odd, isn't it?' Sule glanced at him sharply. 'What's odd about it?' 'You getting stabbed just for asking her to hand over the money.' 'Ask her? I didn't ask her. No earthly use asking anything of characters like that.' 'Oh?' said Dogo. 'I'd always thought all you had to do was ask. True, the coat wasn't yours. But you asked her to sell it. She's an old "fence" and ought to know that you are entitled to the money.' 'Only a fool would be content with fifteen shillings for a coat and a bag,' said Sule. 'And you are not a fool, eh?' chuckled Dogo. 'What did you do about it?' 'Beat the living daylight out of her,' rasped Sule. 'And quite right, too,' commented Dogo. 'Only snag is you seem to have got more than you gave her.' He chuckled again. 'A throbbing wound is no joke,' said Sule testily. 'And who's joking? I've been stabbed in my time, too. You can't go around at night wearing a knife and not expect to get stabbed once in a while. We should regard such things as an occupational hazard.' 'Sure,' grunted Sule. 'But that can't cure a wound.' 'No, but the hospital can,' said Dogo. 'I know. But in the hospital they ask questions before they cure you.'

They were entering the village. In front of them the broad

path diverged into a series of tracks that twined away between the houses. Sule paused, briefly, took one of the paths. They walked along on silent feet, just having a look around. Not a light showed in any of the crowded mud houses. Every little hole of a window was shut or plugged, presumably against the threatening storm. A peal of languid thunder rumbled over from the east. Except for a group of goats and sheep, which rose startled at their approach, the two had the village paths to themselves. Every once in a while Sule would stop by a likely house; the two would take a careful look around; he'd look inquiringly down at his companion, who would shake his head, and they would move on.

They had been walking around for about a quarter of an hour when a brilliant flash of lightning almost burned out their eyeballs. That decided them. 'We'd better hurry,' whispered Dogo. 'The storm's almost here.' Sule said nothing. A dilapidated-looking house stood a few yards away. They walked up to it. They were not put off by its appearance. Experience had taught them that what a house looked like was no indication of what it contained. Some stinking hovels had yielded rich hauls. Dogo nodded at Sule. 'You stay outside and try to keep awake,' said Sule. He nodded at a closed window. 'You might stand near that.'

Dogo moved off to his post. Sule got busy on the crude wooden door. Even Dogo's practised ear did not detect any untoward sound, and from where he stood he couldn't tell when Sule gained entry into the house. He remained at his post for what seemed ages—it was actually a matter of minutes. Presently he saw the window at his side open slowly. He froze against the wall. But it was Sule's muscular hands that came through the window, holding out to him a biggish gourd. Dogo took the gourd and was surprised at its weight. His pulse quickened. People around here trusted gourds like this more than banks. 'The stream,' whispered Sule through the open window. Dogo understood. Hoisting the gourd on to his head, he made off at a fast trot for the stream. Sule would find his way out of the house and follow him.

He set the gourd down carefully by the stream, took off its carved lid. If this contained anything of value, he thought, he and Sule did not have to share it equally. Besides, how did he know Sule had not helped himself to a little of its contents before passing it out through the window? He thrust his right hand into the gourd and next instant he felt a vicious stab on his wrist. A sharp exclamation escaped from him as he jerked his arm out. He peered at his wrist closely then slowly and steadily he began to curse. He damned to hell and glory everything under the sun in the two languages he knew. He sat on the ground, holding his wrist, cursing softly. He heard Sule approaching and stopped. He put the lid back on the gourd and waited. 'Any trouble?' he asked, when the other got to him. 'No trouble,' said Sule. Together they stooped over the gourd. Dogo had to hold his right wrist in his left hand but he did it so Sule wouldn't notice. 'Have you opened it?' Sule asked. 'Who? Me? Oh, no!' said Dogo. Sule did not believe him and he knew it. 'What can be so heavy?' Dogo asked curiously. 'We'll see,' said Sule.

He took off the lid, thrust his hand into the gaping mouth of the gourd and felt a sharp stab on his wrist. He whipped his hand out of the gourd. He stood up. Dogo, too, stood up and for the first time Sule noticed Dogo's wrist held in the other hand. They were silent for a long time, glaring at each other. 'As you always insisted, we should go fifty-fifty in everything,' said Dogo casually. Quietly, almost inaudibly, Sule started speaking. He called Dogo every name known to obscenity. Dogo for his part was holding up his end quite well. They stopped when they had run out of names. 'I am going home,' Dogo announced. 'Wait!' said Sule. With his uninjured hand he rummaged in his pocket, brought out a box of matches. With difficulty he struck one, held the flame over the gourd, peered in. He threw the match away. 'It is not necessary,' he said. 'Why not?' Dogo demanded. 'That in there is an angry cobra,' said Sule. The leaden feeling was creeping up his arm fast. The pain was tremendous. He sat down. 'I still don't see why I can't go home,' said Dogo. 'Have you never heard the saying that what the cobra bites dies at the foot of the cobra? The poison is that good: just perfect for sons of swine like you. You'll never make it home. Better sit down and die here.' Dogo didn't agree but the throbbing pain forced him to sit down.

They were silent for several minutes while the lightning

played around them. Finally Dogo said, 'Funny that your last haul should be a snake-charmer's gourd.' 'I think it's funnier still that it should contain a cobra, don't you?' said Sule. He groaned. 'I reckon funnier things will happen before the night is done,' said Dogo. 'Uh!' he winced with pain. 'A couple of harmless deaths, for instance,' suggested Sule. 'Might as well kill the bloody snake,' said Dogo. He attempted to rise and pick up a stone from the stream; he couldn't. 'Ah, well,' he said, lying on his back. 'It doesn't matter anyway.'

The rain came pattering down. 'But why die in the rain?' he demanded angrily. 'Might help to die soaking wet if you are going straight to hell from here,' said Sule. Teeth clenched, he dragged himself to the gourd, his knife in his good hand. Closing his eyes, he thrust knife and hand into the gourd, drove vicious thrusts into the reptile's writhing body, breathing heavily all the while. When he crawled back to lie down a few minutes later the breath came whistling out of his nostrils; his arm was riddled with fang-marks; but the reptile was dead. 'That's one snake that has been charmed for the last time,' said Sule. Dogo said nothing.

Several minutes passed in silence. The poison had them securely in its fatal grip, especially Sule, who couldn't suppress a few groans. It was only a matter of seconds now. 'Pity you have to end up this way,' mumbled Dogo, his senses dulling. 'By and large, it hasn't been too bad—you thieving scoundrel!' 'I'm soaked in tears on account of you,' drawled Sule, unutterably weary. 'This seems the end of the good old road. But you ought to have known it had to end some time, you rotten bastard!' He heaved a deep sigh. 'I shan't have to go up to the hospital in the morning after all,' he mumbled, touching the wound in his thigh with a trembling hand. 'Ah,' he breathed in resignation, 'the will of Allah be done.' The rain came pattering down.

Civil Peace

Chinua Achebe

Jonathan Iwegbu counted himself extra-ordinarily lucky. 'Happy survival!' meant so much more to him than just a current fashion of greeting old friends in the first hazy days of peace. It went deep to his heart. He had come out of the war with five inestimable blessings—his head, his wife Maria's head and the heads of three out of their four children. As a bonus he also had his old bicycle—a miracle too but naturally not to be compared to the safety of five human heads.

The bicycle had a little history of its own. One day at the height of the war it was commandeered 'for urgent military action'. Hard as its loss would have been to him he would still have let it go without a thought had he not had some doubts about the genuineness of the officer. It wasn't his disreputable rags, nor the toes peeping out of one blue and one brown canvas shoe, nor yet the two stars of his rank done obviously in a hurry in biro, that troubled Jonathan; many good and heroic soldiers looked the same or worse. It was rather a certain lack of grip and firmness in his manner. So Jonathan, suspecting he might be amenable to influence, rummaged in his raffia bag and produced the two pounds with which he had been going to buy firewood which his wife, Maria, retailed to camp officials for extra stock-fish and corn meal, and got his bicycle back. That night he buried it in the little clearing in the bush where the dead of the camp, including his own youngest son, were buried. When he dug it up again a year later after the surrender all it needed was a little palm-oil greasing. 'Nothing puzzles God,' he said in wonder.

He put it to immediate use as a taxi and accumulated a small pile of Biafran money ferrying camp officials and their families across the four-mile stretch to the nearest tarred road. His standard charge per trip was six pounds and those who had the money were only glad to be rid of some of it in this way. At the end of a fortnight he had made a small fortune of one hundred and fifteen pounds.

Then he made the journey to Enugu and found another miracle waiting for him. It was unbelievable. He rubbed his eyes and looked again and it was still standing there before him. But, needless to say, even that monumental blessing must be accounted also totally inferior to the five heads in the family. This newest miracle was his little house in Ogui Overside. Indeed nothing puzzles God! Only two houses away a huge concrete edifice some wealthy contractor had put up just before the war was a mountain of rubble. And here was Jonathan's little zinc house of no regrets built with mud blocks quite intact! Of course the doors and windows were missing and five sheets off the roof. But what was that? And anyhow he had returned to Enugu early enough to pick up bits of old zinc and wood and soggy sheets of cardboard lying around the neighbourhood before thousands more came out of their forest holes looking for the same things. He got a destitute carpenter with one old hammer, a blunt plane and a few bent and rusty nails in his tool bag to turn this assortment of wood, paper and metal into door and window shutters for five Nigerian shillings or fifty Biafran pounds. He paid the pounds, and moved in with his overjoyed family carrying five heads on their shoulders.

His children picked mangoes near the military cemetery and sold them to soldiers' wives for a few pennies—real pennies this time—and his wife started making breakfast akara balls for neighbours in a hurry to start life again. With his family earnings he took his bicycle to the villages around and bought fresh palm-wine which he mixed generously in his rooms with the water which had recently started running again in the public tap down the road, and opened up a bar for soldiers and other lucky people with good money.

At first he went daily, then every other day and finally once a week, to the offices of the Coal Corporation where he used to be a miner, to find out what was what. The only thing he did find out in the end was that that little house of his was even a greater blessing than he had thought. Some of his fellow ex-miners who had nowhere to return at the end of the day's waiting just slept outside the doors of the offices and cooked what meal they could scrounge together in Bournvita tins. As the weeks lengthened and still nobody could say what was what Jonathan discontinued his weekly visits altogether and faced his palm-wine bar.

But nothing puzzles God. Came the day of the windfall when after five days of endless scuffles in queues and counter-queues in the sun outside the Treasury he had twenty pounds counted into his palms as ex-gratia award for the rebel money he had turned in. It was like Christmas for him and for many others like him when the payments began. They called it (since few could manage its proper official name) *egg-rasher*.

As soon as the pound notes were placed in his palm Jonathan simply closed it tight over them and buried fist and money inside his trouser pocket. He had to be extra careful because he had seen a man a couple of days earlier collapse into near-madness in an instant before that oceanic crowd because no sooner had he got his twenty pounds than some heartless ruffian picked it off him. Though it was not right that a man in such an extremity of agony should be blamed yet many in the queues that day were able to remark quietly at the victim's carelessness, especially after he pulled out the innards of his pocket and revealed a hole in it big enough to pass a thief's head. But of course he had insisted that the money had been in the other pocket, pulling it out too to show its comparative wholeness. So one had to be careful.

Jonathan soon transferred the money to his left hand and pocket so as to leave his right free for shaking hands should the need arise, though by fixing his gaze at such an elevation as to miss all approaching human faces he made sure that the need did not arise, until he got home.

He was normally a heavy sleeper but that night he heard all the neighbourhood noises die down one after another. Even the night watchman who knocked the hour on some metal somewhere in the distance had fallen silent after knocking one o'clock. That must have been the last thought in Jonathan's mind before he was finally carried away himself. He couldn't have been gone for long, though, when he was violently awakened again.

'Who is knocking?' whispered his wife lying beside him on the floor.

'I don't know,' he whispered back breathlessly.

The second time the knocking came it was so loud and imperious that the rickety old door could have fallen down.

'Who is knocking?' he asked them, his voice parched and trembling.

'Na tief-man and him people,' came the cool reply. 'Make you hopen de door.' This was followed by the heaviest knocking of all.

Maria was the first to raise the alarm, then he followed and all their children.

'*Police-o! Thieves-o! Neighbours-o! Police-o! We are lost! We are dead! Neighbours, are you asleep? Wake up! Police-o!*'

This went on for a long time and then stopped suddenly. Perhaps they had scared the thief away. There was total silence. But only for a short while.

'You done finish?' asked the voice outside. 'Make we help you small. Oya, everybody!'

'*Police-o! Tief-man-so! Neighbours-o! we done loss-o! Police-o! . . .*'

There were at least five other voices besides the leader's.

Jonathan and his family were now completely paralysed by terror. Maria and the children sobbed inaudibly like lost souls. Jonathan groaned continuously.

The silence that followed the thieves' alarm vibrated horribly. Jonathan all but begged their leader to speak again and be done with it.

'My frien,' said he at long last, 'we don try our best for call dem but I tink say dem all done sleep-o . . . So wetin we go do now? Sometaim you wan call soja? Or you wan make we call dem for you? Soja better pass police. No be so?'

'Na so!' replied his men. Jonathan thought he heard even more voices now than before and groaned heavily. His legs were sagging under him and his throat felt like sandpaper.

'My frien, why you no de talk again. I de ask you say you wan make we call soja?'

'No'.

'Awrighto. Now make we talk business. We no be bad tief. We no like for make trouble. Trouble done finish. War done finish and all the katakata wey de for inside. No Civil War again. This time na Civil Peace. No be so?'

'Na so!' answered the horrible chorus.

'What do you want from me? I am a poor man. Everything I had went with this war. Why do you come to me? You know people who have money. We . . .'

'Awright! We know say you no get plenty money. But we sef no get even anini. So derefore make you open dis window and give us one hundred pound and we go commot. Orderwise we de come for inside now to show you guitar-boy like dis . . .'

A volley of automatic fire rang through the sky. Maria and the children began to weep aloud again.

'Ah, missisi de cry again. No need for dat. We done talk say we na good tief. We just take our small money and go nwayorly. No molest. Abi we de molest?'

'At all!' sang the chorus.

'My friends,' began Jonathan hoarsely. 'I hear what you say and I thank you. If I had one hundred pounds . . .'

'Lookia my frien, no be play we come play for your house. If we make mistake and step for inside you no go like am-o. So derefore . . .'

'To God who made me; if you come inside and find one hundred pounds, take it and shoot me and shoot my wife and children. I swear to God. The only money I have in this life is this twenty-pounds *egg-rasher* they gave me today . . .'

'Ok. Time de go. Make you open dis window and bring the twenty pound. We go manage am like dat.'

There were now loud murmurs of dissent among the chorus: 'Na lie de man de lie; e get plenty money . . . Make we go inside and search properly well . . . Wetin be twenty pound? . . .'

'Shurrup!' rang the leader's voice like a lone shot in the sky and silenced the murmuring at once. 'Are you dere? Bring the money quick!'

'I am coming,' said Jonathan fumbling in the darkness with the key of the small wooden box he kept by his side on the mat.

At the first sign of light as neighbours and others assembled to commiserate with him he was already strapping his five-gallon demijohn to his bicycle carrier and his wife, sweating in the open fire, was turning over akara balls in a wide clay bowl of boiling oil. In the corner his eldest son was rinsing out dregs of yesterday's palm-wine from old beer bottles.

'I count it as nothing,' he told his sympathizers, his eyes on the rope he was tying. 'What is *egg-rasher*? Did I depend on it last week? Or is it greater than other things that went with the war? I say, let *egg-rasher* perish in the flames! Let it go where everything else has gone. Nothing puzzles God.'

EAST AFRICA

The Gentlemen of the Jungle

Jomo Kenyatta

Once upon a time an elephant made a friendship with a man. One day a heavy thunderstorm broke out, the elephant went to his friend, who had a little hut at the edge of the forest, and said to him: 'My dear good man, will you please let me put my trunk inside your hut to keep it out of this torrential rain?' The man, seeing what situation his friend was in, replied: 'My dear good elephant, my hut is very small, but there is room for your trunk and myself. Please put your trunk in gently.' The elephant thanked his friend, saying: 'You have done me a good deed and one day I shall return your kindness.' But what followed? As soon as the elephant put his trunk inside the hut, slowly he pushed his head inside, and finally flung the man out in the rain, and then lay down comfortably inside his friend's hut, saying: 'My dear good friend, your skin is harder than mine, and as there is not enough room for both of us, you can afford to remain in the rain while I am protecting my delicate skin from the hailstorm.'

The man, seeing what his friend had done to him, started to grumble; the animals in the nearby forest heard the noise and came to see what was the matter. All stood around listening to the heated argument between the man and his friend the elephant. In this turmoil the lion came along roaring, and said in a loud voice: 'Don't you all know that I am the King of the Jungle! How dare any one disturb the peace of my kingdom?' On hearing this the elephant, who was one of the high ministers in the jungle kingdom, replied in a soothing voice, and said: 'My lord, there is no disturbance of the peace in your kingdom. I have only been having a little discussion with my friend here as to the possession of this little hut which your lordship sees me occupying.' The lion, who wanted to have 'peace and tranquillity' in his kingdom, replied in a noble voice, saying: 'I command my ministers to appoint a Commission of Enquiry to go thoroughly into this matter and report accordingly.' He then turned to the man and said: 'You have done well by establishing friendship with my people, especially with the elephant, who is one of my honourable ministers of state. Do not grumble any more, your hut is not lost to you. Wait until the sitting of my Imperial Commission, and there you will be given plenty of opportunity to state your case. I am sure that you will be pleased with the findings of the Commission.' The man was very pleased by these sweet words from the King of the Jungle, and innocently waited for his opportunity, in the belief that naturally the hut would be returned to him.

The elephant, obeying the command of his master, got busy with other ministers to appoint the Commission of Enquiry. The following elders of the jungle were appointed to sit in the Commission: (1) Mr Rhinoceros; (2) Mr Buffalo; (3) Mr Alligator; (4) The Rt Hon. Mr Fox to act as chairman; and (5) Mr Leopard to act as Secretary to the Commission. On seeing the personnel, the man protested and asked if it was not necessary to include in this Commission a member from his side. But he was told that it was impossible, since no one from his side was well enough educated to understand the intricacy of jungle law. Further, that there was nothing to fear, for the members of the Commission were all men of repute for their impartiality in justice, and as they were gentlemen chosen by God to look after the interests of races less adequately endowed with teeth and claws, he might rest assured that they would investigate the matter with the greatest care and report impartially.

The Commission sat to take the evidence. The Rt Hon. Mr Elephant was first called. He came along with a superior air, brushing his tusks with a sapling which Mrs Elephant had provided, and in an authoritative voice said: 'Gentlemen of the Jungle, there is no need for me to waste your valuable time in relating a story which I am sure you all know. I have always regarded it as my duty to protect the interests of my friends, and this appears to have caused the misunderstanding between myself and my friend here. He invited me to save his hut from being blown away by a hurricane. As the hurricane had gained access owing to the unoccupied space in the hut, I considered it necessary, in my friend's own interests, to turn the undeveloped space to a more economic use by sitting in it myself; a duty which any of you would undoubtedly have performed with equal readiness in similar circumstances.'

After hearing the Rt Hon. Mr Elephant's conclusive evidence, the Commission called Mr Hyena and other elders of the jungle, who all supported what Mr Elephant had said. They then called the man, who began to give his own account of the dispute. But the Commission cut him short, saying: 'My good man, please confine yourself to relevant issues. We have already heard the circumstances from various unbiased sources; all we wish you to tell us is whether the undeveloped space in your hut was occupied by any one else before Mr Elephant assumed his position?' The man began to say: 'No, but—' But at this point the Commission declared that they had heard sufficient evidence from both sides and retired to consider their decision. After enjoying a delicious meal at the expense of the Rt Hon. Mr Elephant, they reached their verdict, called the man, and declared as follows: 'In our opinion this dispute has arisen through a regrettable misunderstanding due to the backwardness of your ideas. We consider that Mr Elephant has fulfilled his sacred duty of protecting your interests. As it is clearly for your good that the space should be put to its most economic use, and as you yourself have not reached the stage of expansion which would enable you to fill it, we consider it necessary to arrange a compromise to suit both parties. Mr Elephant shall continue his occupation of your hut, but we give you permission to look for a site where you can build another hut more suited to your needs, and we will see that you are well protected.'

The man, having no alternative, and fearing that his refusal might expose him to the teeth and claws of members of the Commission, did as they suggested. But no sooner had he built another hut than Mr Rhinoceros charged in with his horn lowered and ordered the man to quit. A Royal Commission was again appointed to look into the matter, and the same finding was given. This procedure was repeated until Mr Buffalo, Mr Leopard, Mr Hyena and the rest were all accommodated with new huts. Then the man decided that he must adopt an effective method of protection, since Commissions of Enquiry did not seem to be of any use to him. He sat down and said, *'Ng'enda thi ndagaga motegi,'* which literally means 'there is nothing that treads on the earth that cannot be trapped,' or in other words, you can fool people for a time, but not for ever.

Early one morning, when the huts already occupied by the jungle lords were all beginning to decay and fall to pieces, he went out and built a bigger and better hut a little distance away. No sooner had Mr Rhinoceros seen it than he came rushing in, only to find that Mr Elephant was already inside, sound asleep. Mr Leopard next came to the window, Mr Lion, Mr Fox and Mr Buffalo entered the doors, while Mr Hyena howled for a place in the shade and Mr Alligator basked on the roof. Presently they all began disputing about their rights of penetration, and from disputing they came to fighting, and while they were all embroiled together the man set the hut on fire and burnt it to the ground, jungle lords and all. Then he went home, saying: 'Peace is costly, but it's worth the expense,' and lived happily ever after.

The Green Leaves

Grace Ogot

It was a dream. Then the sounds grew louder. Nyagar threw the blanket off his ears and listened. Yes, he was right. Heavy footsteps and voices were approaching. He turned round to wake up his wife. She was not there. He got up and rushed to the door. It was unlocked. Where was Nyamundhe? 'How could she slip back to her hut so quietly?' he wondered. 'I've told her time and again never to leave my hut without waking me up to bolt the door. She will see me tomorrow!'

'*Ero, ero*, there, there!' The noise was quite close now— about thirty yards away. Nyagar put a sheet round his well-developed body, fumbled for his spear and club, and then left the hut.

'*Piti, piti. Piti, piti.*' A group was running towards his gate. He opened the gate and hid by the fence. Nyagar did not want to meet the group directly, as he was certain some dangerous person was being pursued.

Three or four men ran past the gate, and then a larger group followed. He emerged from his hiding-place and followed them.

'These bastards took all my six bulls,' he heard one voice cursing.

'Don't worry—they will pay for it,' another voice replied.

Nyagar had caught up with the pursuing crowd. He now realised that the three or four men he had seen run past his gate were cattle thieves. They rounded a bend. About thirty yards away were three figures who could only be the thieves.

'They must not escape,' a man shouted.

'They will not,' the crowd answered in chorus.

The gap was narrowing. The young moon had disappeared, and it was quite dark.

'Don't throw a spear,' an elder warned. 'If it misses, they can use it against us.'

The thieves took the wrong turning. They missed the bridge across the River Opok, which separated the people of Masala from those of Mirogi. Instead they turned right. While attempting to cross the river, they suddenly found themselves in a whirlpool. Hastily they scrambled out of the water.

'*Ero, ero,*' a cry went out from the pursuers.

Before the thieves could find a safe place at which to cross the river, the crowd was upon them. With their clubs they smote the thieves to the ground. The air was filled with the howls of the captured men. But the crowd showed no mercy.

During the scuffle, one of the thieves escaped and disappeared into the thick bush by the river.

'Follow him! Follow him!' someone shouted.

Three men ran in the direction in which he had disappeared, breathing heavily. The bush was thick and thorny. They stood still and listened. There was no sound. They beat the bush around with their clubs—still no sound. He had escaped.

Another thief took out his knife and drove it into the shoulder-blade of one of the pursuers, who fell back with the knife still sticking in him. In the ensuing confusion, the thief got up and made straight for the whirlpool. To everybody's amazement, he was seen swimming effortlessly across it to the other side of the river.

Nyagar plucked the knife out from Omoro's shoulder and put his hand over the wound to stop the bleeding. Omoro, still shaken, staggered to his feet and leaned on Nyagar. Streaks of blood were still running along his back, making his buttocks wet.

One thief was lying on the grass, groaning. As the other two had escaped, the crowd were determined to make an example of this one. They hit him several times on the head and chest. He groaned and stretched out his arms and legs as if giving up the ghost.

'Aa, aa,' Omoro raised his voice. 'Let not the enemy die in your hands. His spirit would rest upon our village. Let him give up the ghost when we have returned to our huts.'

The crowd heeded Omoro's warning. They tore green leaves from nearby trees and covered the victim completely with them. They would call the entire clan in the morning to come and bury him by the riverside.

The men walked back home in silence. Omoro's shoulder had stopped bleeding. He walked, supported by two friends who volunteered to take him home. It was still not light, but their eyes were by now accustomed to the darkness. They reached Nyagar's home—the gate was still ajar.

'Remember to be early tomorrow,' a voice told him. 'We must be on the scene to stop the women before they start going to the river.'

Nyagar entered his home, while the others walked on without looking back. The village was hushed. The women must have been awake, but they dared not talk to their husbands. Whatever had happened, they thought, they would hear about it in the morning. Having satisfied themselves that their husbands were safely back, they turned over and slept.

Nyagar entered his hut, searched for his medicine bag and found it in a corner. He opened it, and pulled out a bamboo container. He uncorked the container, and then scooped out some ash from it. He placed a little on his tongue, mixed it well with saliva and then swallowed. He put some on his palm and blew it in the direction of the gate. As he replaced the bamboo container in the bag, his heart felt at peace.

He sat on the edge of his bed. He started to remove his clothes. Then he changed his mind. Instead he just sat there, staring vacantly into space. Finally he made up his mind to go back to the dead man alone.

He opened the door slowly, and then closed it quietly after him. No one must hear him.

He did not hesitate at the gate, but walked blindly on.

'Did I close the gate?' he wondered. He looked back. Yes, he had closed it—or it looked closed.

Apart from a sinister sound which occasionally rolled through the night, everything was silent. Dawn must have been approaching. The faint and golden gleams of light which usually herald the birth of a new day could be seen in the east shooting skywards from the bowels of the earth. 'He must have a lot of money in his pocket,' Nyagar said aloud. He knew that stock thieves sold stolen cattle at the earliest opportunity.

'The others were foolish not to have searched him.' He stopped and listened. Was somebody coming? No. He was merely hearing the echo of his own footsteps.

'Perhaps the other two thieves who had escaped are now back at the scene,' he thought nervously. 'No, they can't be there—they wouldn't be such idiots as to hang around there.'

The heap of green leaves came in sight. A numb paralysing pain ran through his spine. He thought his heart had stopped beating. He stopped to check. It was still beating, all right. He was just nervous. He moved on faster, and the echo of his footsteps bothered him.

When Nyagar reached the scene of murder, he noticed that everything was exactly as they had left it earlier. He stood there for a while, undecided. He looked in all directions to ensure that no one was coming. There was nobody. He was all alone with the dead body. He now felt nervous. 'Why should you disturb a dead body?' his inner voice asked him. 'What do you want to do with money? You have three wives and twelve children. You have many cattle and enough food. What more do you want?' the voice persisted. He felt even more nervous, and was about to retreat when an urge stronger than his will egged him on.

'You have come all this far for one cause only, and the man is lying before you. You only need to put your hand in his pockets, and all the money will be yours. Don't deceive yourself that you have enough wealth. Nobody in the world has enough wealth.'

Nyagar bent over the dead man, and hurriedly removed the leaves from him. His hand came in contact with the man's arm which lay folded on his chest. It was still warm. A chill ran through him again, and he stood up. It was unusual for a dead person to be warm, he thought. However, he dismissed the thought. Perhaps he was just nervous and was imagining things. He bent over the man again, and rolled him on his back. He looked dead all right.

He fumbled quickly to find the pockets. He dipped his hand into the first pocket. It was empty. He searched the second pocket—that, too, was empty. A pang of disappointment ran through his heart. Then he remembered that cattle traders often carried their money in a small bag stringed with a cord round their neck.

He knelt beside the dead man and found his neck. Sure enough there was a string tied around his neck, from which hung a little bag. A triumphant smile played at the corners of his mouth. Since he had no knife with which to cut the string, he decided to remove it over the man's head. As Nyagar lifted the man's head, there was a crashing blow on his right eye. He staggered for a few yards and fell unconscious to the ground.

The thief had just regained consciousness and was still very weak. But there was no time to lose. He managed to get up on his feet after a second attempt. His body was soaked in blood, but his mind was now clear. He gathered all the green leaves and heaped them on Nyagar. He then made for the bridge which he had failed to locate during the battle.

He walked away quickly—the spirit should not leave the body while he was still on the scene. It was nearly dawn. He would reach the river Migua in time to rinse the blood off his clothes.

Before sunrise, the clan leader Olielo sounded the funeral drum to alert the people. Within an hour more than a hundred clansmen had assembled at the foot of the *Opok* tree where the elders normally met to hear criminal and civil cases. Olielo then addressed the gathering.

'Listen, my people. Some of you must have heard of the trouble we had in our clan last night. Thieves broke into Omogo's kraal and stole six of his ploughing oxen.'

'Oh!' the crowd exclaimed.

Olielo continued, 'As a result, blood was shed, and we now have a body lying here.'

'Is this so?' one elder asked.

'Yes, it is so,' Olielo replied. 'Now listen to me. Although our laws prohibit any wanton killing, thieves and adulterers we regard as animals. If anyone kills one of them he is not guilty of murder. He is looked upon as a person who has rid society of an evil spirit, and in return society has a duty to protect him and his children. You all know that such a person must be cleansed before he again associates with other members of society. But the white man's laws are different. According to his laws, if you kill a man because you find him stealing your cattle or sleeping in your wife's hut, you are guilty of murder—and therefore you must also be killed. Because he thinks his laws are superior to ours, we should handle him carefully. We have ancestors—the white man has none. That is why they bury their dead far away from their houses.

'This is what we should do. We shall send thirty men to the white man to tell him that we have killed a thief. This group should tell him that the whole clan killed the thief. Take my word, my children. The white man's tricks work only among a divided people. If we stand united, none of us will be killed.'

'The old man has spoken well,' they shouted. Thirty men were elected, and they immediately left for the white man's camp.

More people, including some women, had arrived to swell the number of the group. They moved towards the river where the dead thief lay covered in leaves, to await the arrival of the white man.

Nyamundhe moved near her co-wife. 'Where is Nyagar? My eye has not caught him.'

His co-wife peered through the crowd, and then answered, 'I think he has gone with the thirty. He left home quite early. I woke up very early this morning, but the gate was open. He had left the village.'

Nyamundhe recollected that as they entered the narrow path which led to the river, their feet felt wet from the morning dew. And bending across the path as if saying prayers to welcome the dawn, were long grasses which were completely overpowered by the thick dew. She wanted to ask her co-wife where their husband could have gone but, noticing her indifference, she had decided to keep quiet.

'I did not like that black cat which dashed in front of us when we were coming here,' Nyamundhe said to her co-wife.

'Yes, it is a bad sign for a black cat to cross one's way first thing in the morning.'

They heard the sound of a lorry. They looked up and saw a cloud of dust and two police lorries approaching.

The two lorries pulled up by the heap of green leaves A European police officer and four African officers stepped down. They opened the back of one of the lorries and the thirty men who had been sent to the police station by the clan came out.

'Where is the clan elder?' the white officer demanded.

Olielo stepped forward.

'Tell me the truth. What happened? I don't believe a word of what these people are saying. What did you send them to tell me?'

Olielo spoke sombrely and slowly in Dholuo, pronouncing every word distinctly. His words were translated by an African police officer.

'I sent them to inform you that we killed a thief last night.'

'What! You killed a man?' the white man moved towards Olielo. The other policeman followed him.

'You killed a man?' the white officer repeated.

'No, we killed a thief.' Olielo maintained his ground.

'How many times have I told you that you must abandon this savage custom of butchering one another? No one is a thief until he has been tried in a court of law and found guilty. Your people are deaf.' The white man pointed at Olielo with his stick in an ominous manner.

'This time I shall show you how to obey the law. Who killed him?' the white officer asked angrily.

'All of us,' answered Olielo, pointing at the crowd.

'Don't be silly. Who hit him first?'

The crowd was getting restless. The people surged forward menacingly towards the five police officers.

'We all hit the thief,' they shouted.

'If you want to arrest us, you are free to do so. You'd better send for more lorries.'

'Where is the dead man?' the white man asked Olielo.

'There,' Olielo replied, pointing at the heap of leaves.

The police moved towards the heap. The crowd also pushed forward. They wanted to get a glimpse of him before the white man took him away.

The last time a man had been killed in the area, the police took the corpse to Kisumu where it was cut up into pieces and then stiched up again. Then they returned it to the people saying, 'Here is your man—bury him.' Some people claimed that bile is extracted from such bodies and given to police tracker dogs; and that is why the dogs can track a thief to his house. Many people believed such stories. They were sure that this body would be taken away again by the police.

The European officer told the other police officer to uncover the body. They hesitated for a while, and then obeyed.

Olielo looked at the body before them unbelievingly. Then he looked at his people, and at the police. Was he normal? Where was the thief? He looked at the body a second time. He was not insane. It was the body of Nyagar, his cousin, who lay dead, with a sizable wooden stick driven through his right eye.

Nyamundhe broke loose from the crowd and ran towards the dead body. She fell on her husband's body and wept bitterly. Then turning to the crowd, she shouted, 'Where is the thief you killed? Where is he?'

As the tension mounted, the crowd broke up into little groups of twos and threes. The women started to wail; and the men who had killed the thief that night looked at one another in complete disbelief. They had left Nyagar entering his village while they walked on. They could swear to it. Then Olielo, without any attempt to conceal his tear-drenched face, appealed to his people with these words, 'My countrymen, the evil hand has descended upon us. Let it not break up our society. Although Nyagar is dead, his spirit is still among us.'

But Nyamundhe did not heed the comforts of Jaduong' Olielo nor did she trust the men who swore that they had seen Nyagar enter his village after the incident with the thieves. She struggled wildly with the police who carried the corpse of her husband and placed it on the back of the lorry to be taken to Kisumu for a post-mortem. A police officer comforted her with the promise that a village-wide-enquiry would start at once into the death of her husband.

But Nyamundhe shook her head. 'If you say you will give him back to me alive, then I will listen.'

Nyamundhe tore her clothes and stripped to the waist. She walked slowly behind the mourners, weeping and chanting, her hands raised above her head.

> My lover the son of Ochieng'
> The son of Omolo
> The rains are coming down
> Yes, the rains are coming down

The nights will be dark
The nights will be cold and long.
Oh! the son-in-law of my mother
I have no heart to forgive,
I have no heart to pardon
All these mourners cheat me now
Yes, they cheat me
But when the sun goes to his home and
Darkness falls, they desert me.
In the cold hours of the night
Each woman clings to her man
There is no one among them
There is none
There is no woman who will lend me a
Husband for the night
Ah, my lover, the son of Ochieng'
The son-law of my mother.

Bossy

Abdulrazak Gurnah

A long time ago that was, sitting on the barnacled pier, swinging our legs through the air. Princess Margaret pier in the long shadow of the afternoon, watching the sea beneath us frothing with arms and legs and flashing teeth. A long story I told him, urbane and wise, a fabric of lies. I told him of a man who stood by the sea and peed, and how his pee was continuous without end. Like the tongue of infinite length, all coiled up in a man's insides. On Princess Margaret pier we watched Ferej eat up the water like a shark. The water choppy and bright on the day he won the schools' championship. On Princess Margaret pier, after a day in 1956 when the good princess laid foot on our humble land. On the other side were four guns, riveted into the concrete and facing the sea. Ceremonial fire-crackers to bid the princess welcome.

The letter had arrived that morning, a dirty scrap to shatter my self-inflicted peace. Karim's name was written clearly on the back of the air mail form, and all the remaining space was covered with hand-written HAPPY NEW YEAR wishes.

31 December 1973

Dear Haji,

(O Pilgrim to the Promised Land)

I am sitting inside our office, or to be more precise, our storeroom, being entertained by the sounds of the sawing, planing, sanding and drilling machines. Together with the rhythmic tapping of hammers on nails, all this combines to form a unique masterpiece at the eleventh hour of the year The prevailing atmosphere has nothing to do with my writing to you, but just to deliver that presently I am indentured to a cyclops by name Rahman whose cave this Wood-Works is. I guess you will be surprised to hear that I am also concubined to his daughter.

You may also be surprised to hear that today I am celebrating my first 'Go West Young Man' anniversary. It is only twenty miles west, but you know how big that distance really is. Exactly a year ago, on a Sunday afternoon, myself along with some other freedom lovers were preparing to act and follow that great genius, master and generator of electricity, the organiser and pilot of our expedition, Captain-General Jabir Dumas (also well known as Hamlet of ST 9 fame). Between you and me, I learned the identity of the master-mind too late to retreat, just when the sail was being hoisted in fact. But before we could wave fond goodbye to the dear homeland, forever verdant and green, we were tackled by a wandering varantia. It needed a hefty bribe to fix him. We had a hazardous journey, during which it was apparent that our Hamlet did not know southerly from a handsaw. However, we landed on a beach which turned out to be some eighty miles north of our destination. Once we'd landed, the journey was smooth and easy, and I shall remain content to say that we arrived here tired but in one piece. So much for the forced adventure.

What has been happening to you over the last year? Your silence seems to grow deeper with time. Your last letter contained only one line, and I did not even understand it. Are you still working or have you found a University place yet? Write and tell me how you are doing buddy. I want to hear about all those females who are keeping you busy. Send me a snapshot if you can. I want to see if you have got any fatter.

I have been continuing with my studies in evening classes. It's damned hard work getting back from the mill and going straight to college. As you might guess, I am not doing very well. I have to attend every evening. I start work at seven in the morning which doesn't leave much time for studying at home. Still, nothing ventured: I have become very interested in the poetry of the French Symbolists, but as you know it's not easy to get books here. If you see anything along those lines, I would be very grateful if you would send it to me. Refund by pigeon-post. You know, I miss all those conversations we used to have. There's no one here to talk to, not seriously anyway. People just want to talk about who has been caught fiddling with government funds.

A lot of the pals from home are here now. Hassan was caught trying to escape with some Goan girls in a ngarawa. They were kept for a few days, then released, nobody knows why. Hassan somehow managed to find another way of escaping and he too is here now. The Barrister has gone to a University in Boston to do Intentional Chemistry. Don't ask me, that's what he said. I met his brother recently and he told me that our Barrister is paid a lot of dollar by the American government, who are also paying his fees. So I am thinking of applying to Uncle Sam too.

Did you have a nice Christmas? It was very quiet here except Bachu got drunk and started calling our island leader 'ham-neck'. Poor fellow got kicked out of his office for calling his boss a donkey. Incidentally, do you remember Amina Marehemu Rashid's sister? She must have been about ten when you left. She is now a prostitute. No more room. Write soon and don't forget the snap. Regards from all the pals.

Yours,
Karim.

Gleeful tallysheet of past misdeeds. A time there was . . . but we ended it all with a careless selfishness. Now a fool with a poor style can make fun of your sister. He wants me to send him books of the French Symbolists because he can't get them out there. You missed the worst, Rashid. You missed the worst, my Bossy. Your sister appears as a footnote and not a tear shed for her. You too, you and I we would have watched while a neighbour turned beggar and sold his daughter for shark-meat. And we too would have laughed. All they taught us was how to be meek while they rode rough-shod. You and I, we had something. . . In this cold and often hostile place I often think of you. It was a morning in December that I first wept for you. But by then that heartless land had turned your blood to dust.

It was a beautiful morning in December, bone dry and hot.

We went to borrow a boat to go sailing because we were bored with being on holiday with nothing to do. He went one way, I went the other. He got a boat. I didn't.

'This is your captain speaking,' he said, assuming command.

When he saw that I wasn't going to argue, he suggested that we go and find somebody else to go with us. At that very minute a fellow called Yunis appeared and we struggled into the outrigger and pushed off before he could come and talk to us. Yunis was nicknamed Wire because it was quite obvious that he had some wires disconnected in his head. He was harmless enough but he had allowed this idiocy of his to go to his head. A little guilty I watched him standing on Ras Matengo looking our way. He was probably used to people running away from him.

Before I got to know Rashid well, Wire and I used to spend a lot of time together. He told me about his crazy projects and I told him about mine. He was going to build a ship and sail it himself. He possessed several manuals on ship-building and navigation. The people at the shipping control office knew him well and called him captain to please him. Wire never seemed to listen when you talked to him and even little children could bully him. I saw a little boy of six pee in his mouth once while he was lying in the shade of a tree. Without saying a word, Wire had stood up and left. The adults watching had laughed and patted the boy on the back. I have seen Wire walking past a group of youths lathering at the mouth with fear. But under the line of trees by the dockside, very few people bothered us. We started a club the two of us. It was really a prisoner-of-war camp. I was a major and he was, of course, a captain. I boasted to him about how well I was doing at school and he lied to me about his father's estates in India.

His father lived in one of the houses my father owned. It was supposed to be a shop and apparently was at one time a thriving shop. But as far as I can remember, all it ever had were boxes of rusty nails and showcases with old fishing hooks and twine. If anybody stopped to buy anything from the shop, Wire's father would ask them to lend him some money. He went to the mosque every day, five times a day, and always asked somebody for money. He did the rounds of his neighbours and asked them for money. He went to the welfare office and asked them for money. I don't know if he made any money from all this, but I know he never paid my father any rent. He was thin and small and the skin on his cheeks was leathery and flabby. His jaw was sunken because he had no teeth left. Wire told me that he had large estates in India but he did not have enough money for the journey back home. Wire would build a ship and take his family back home. In the meantime his father tried to persuade him to take a job, but Wire always refused on the grounds that then he would not be able to continue with his maritime studies.

I watched him standing at the water's edge on Ras Matengo and remembered the times we used to sit under the line of trees and eat rotten fruit and stolen biscuits. My parents were worried then, they thought I too had a screw missing. I watched the idiot standing at the brink, watching us sailing to his father's estates in India.

Rashid was laughing, saying what a close call that was. In full sight of the beach Rashid began to imitate Wire's mad mannerisms. He folded his legs under him and rocked his trunk backwards and forwards in a steady rhythm. Wire used to do that when he was young, for hours on end. He was watching us with a smile. He smiled and waved and turned to go.

'What did you do that for?' I said to Rashid.

He ignored me and peeled his shirt off. I think he was ashamed of my former friendship with Wire.

'Let's get cracking,' he said, 'if you want to get to the island and back in time for dinner.'

Bossy was in his element. I knew nothing about boats and he was an expert. He was also a champion swimmer, a national record-holder over 400 metres. He was a footballer with a future and a very useful slow left-arm bowler. He was fair skinned and handsome and wore a wristwatch with a silver strap. It was given to him by the English Club for taking seven of their wickets for 23 runs. To begin with I was proud to be his friend, but over the years we have got to know each other and he has stopped bossing me around.

My god, it hurts to talk like this, as if what has happened had not happened. Bossy and I walked the streets in tandem. We wrote love letters to Hakim and signed them Carol and watched him strut and preen and boast of a secret admirer. We even arranged meetings between him and 'Carol' and always cancelled them at the last minute. Bossy and I spent many dark hours by the cricket ground talking about the future and the past.

On that day in December we set off for Prison Island. The island had been used briefly by the British as a jail. There was now only the perimeter of the camp left. It was a beautiful island, with gently rolling hills and underground springs bubbling into streams. It was off bounds to visitors but nobody took any notice.

The sail on the outrigger caught the breeze and we slipped over the water with only a faint tearing sound. The sea was calm and blue under the morning light, and Rashid started to sing. He sang very badly and did it to provoke laughter more than anything else. He turned to look back towards land. I remember that because then he turned round to me and said didn't it look beautiful from here. It was calm and peaceful and the breeze was just enough to keep the boat moving and us cool. But there was something else. You felt that somehow you had got away from a suffocating room and you were now running free in an open field. The water was cool, as you might imagine water to be, not like the lukewarm water out of a tap. It was the town that looked unreal, like a quaint model in a builder's office. Out here it did not matter that the trousers did not fit, that your skin was fair or dark. There were no smelly alleys to walk through, no slippery ditches to cross, no fanatical and self-righteous elders to humiliate you. There were not even women to taunt you with their bodies beyond your reach.

'I can't just leave Mama and Amina,' said Rashid.

His father had died a couple of years previously. In the Msikiti Mdogo I had stood at a distance and watched him calmly performing the duties of a bereaved son. He walked around amongst the mourners, accepting the condolences of neighbours and strangers with a dry face. I wished he would shed a few tears, for his own sake. It doesn't look good when a sixteen year old can go to his father's funeral with a dry face.

Afterwards he said that he did not cry because he had felt nothing inside. He had wanted to feel sad that his father had died but instead he felt only responsibility. He said his father had been cruel and distant to him ever since he could remember. And now he was really quite relieved that the old bastard had died. I said you can't hold that sort of thing against a dead man. So he smiled his tolerant big brother smile at me and asked who he should hold it against then. I told him that a dead man needed our prayers and he said that prayers would not do that old fucker any good at all. He said the angels of hell must be rubbing their hands at the prospect of his arrival. I said it didn't seem right to talk about your father like that. He said I did not understand because I had a kind father who cared about me and took an interest in me. I said it still didn't seem right to want him to go to hell. He was silent for a long while then told me that there was no hell. And here I told him that he was wrong.

'I can't just leave them on their own,' he said. 'What will they do? What will they do on their own?'

'You won't be gone forever,' I said. 'You'll be back to care for them.'

'Mama is getting old,' he said. 'What's the use of me going away somewhere for five or six years to become a forestry officer only to come back and find that my mother is dead and my sister is a whore.'

'Don't bullshit, Bossy,' I said.

'Okay,' he said, 'maybe I'm not painting it too bright.'

I told him that his tone reminded me of Mundhir's painting of the Black Sea.

Ancient perambulator of a seaward elitat. Velvet blue waist coasts and dark green metal rims waving from the steamer. Buibui on a waterborne outing with a crowd of ragamuffins to serve the sweetmeat. Out for the day with muscular chaperones and camera clicking siblings.

At the island.

Improvised louver in the bush for temporary lordosis with bent knees.

Hasty dunking on the treacherously sandbanked beach to wash the crumbs away and depart for the crumbling fortress of a bygone empire.

Bygone by name.

Over the remains Bossy read the Psalm of Life and lingered meaningfully over dust to dust and sang 'Rule Brittania' with an emotional choke. Lest there be any mistaking his intention, he waved two fingers in benediction.

Deadwood remnants at the camp of the trivial offender against the crown. At the word of command the salvo blew the cheeks apart. That will teach the silly bugger to pay his taxes next time.

Deadwood remnants of pillar post contumelia in thatch-wood alcoves in Indonesian plan.

Over the water turned to dust and a musical lyre was found by the British Archaeological Expedition to the eastern coast of Africa in 1929 to clinch the theory of an Indonesian invasion plan. Fragments of skull found by Blunt KCMG at the lip of the gully to suggest human life before the beginning of time. As counted from the eighth millennium BC. Before that do not apply.

In Blunt Gully Bossy louvered again and nearly choked from the smell.

In a grotto of palms choked with weeds and wild tomatoes we discovered an underground town. We were not welcome and hurried from fierce mandibles until weakened by fatigue and hunger we collapsed under a mango tree which we immediately named Out of Town.

Pungent leaf mould and rotting humus and ripe mangoes oozing on the ground. Bossy bigboots was voted upstairs to wheedle bounty for the starving vanguard of a civilising race. Mangoes on the ground in torpid contentment, oozing like dysentry in harmony with the flies. The captain returned with phosphates in his eyes, the bounty of a discordant piebald crow. We sank to our knees in humiliating penance and fought for mangoes with the flies. God was on our side.

Bossy bigboots brushed the dirt off his booty while hygiene rang through my skull.

I held Hunger in Abeyance and warned Bossy that by Avarice he was undone.

O Mummy in my heart, I prayed, if ever I needed you it is now. Tell me truly, O Fount of Hygiene, will I sooner die of Hunger or of Dysentry. O Wiper of my Arse, I have heeded your word through Thick and Thin generally speaking, but now a Text sirens through my guts to throw Caution to the winds. Could it be the Serpent, viper vile, that so flatters me to eat against your word? To a thicket I slunk and guilty rash gorged of the forbidden fruit. Earth trembled from her entrails but I took no thought content to eat my fill.

Faint rumble pinpoint umbilical cord, distant flutter in the heart. I knelt down waiting for the thunder to strike, and Bossy looked on with pagan amazement. Mother Hygiene restrained her hand. We left that pernicious grotto myself restrained and chastened, Bossy exultant and full.

To the waterfall.

It seemed then that there ought to be a watermill as a sign of progress and evidence of an ancient Indonesian culture. Feet in the pool at the bottom, kicking the water in adolescent delight. We drank the water at our feet, walked to the slimy rocks midpool like rising crustaceans covered with slime. We posed for a photo to show the folks back home hand on hip.

This rock we named Bygone My Arse.

As we sat under that rippling fall, I gazed in wonder at what the old voyagers must have seen. In this same place an Indonesian sultan must have stood with the power of the human gaze to tear holes through nature's incomprehensible veil. Bear thee up Bossy and trust the power of thy unflinching gaze. How many men had stood where you and I then stood and saw nothing of what we saw? We were God's chosen few . . . and we sat by the brimming pool and saw world without end in our humble reflections . . . in foolish daydream pretence. The words of dead past masters ringing anvils to stiffen our self-esteem.

But soon it was time to leave the heaven of that waterfall encampment for the final leg of our journey. Bossy took the lead while I patrolled the rear. As I watched him cut his way through the thicket I wondered again at the destiny that the Almighty had arranged for us. But come what may, I knew that we had done our share in fulfilling the burden of our race. Notwithstanding. Around.

We got back to the beach where we had left the outrigger and went in for a swim. At least Bossy did while I stood in water waist deep and washed the grime off my body.

'Don't show off,' I shouted to him.

He waved back, turned to face the beach and came in at a sprint. I told him he was a bighead and he just grinned contentedly. We sat on the beach to dry off and he told me that he could swim back to town quicker than I could sail the boat back. He was always boasting like that and I just said yeah.

'You don't believe me?' he asked.

'I believe you Bossy,' I said. Now stop mucking around.

It was getting late in the afternoon and I suggested that we make our way back. We turned the boat round and pushed it out to sea. I jumped into it first and helped Bossy in. As soon as we'd hoisted the sail, Bossy stood up, said goodbye and jumped overboard.

'See you in town,' he said, grinning in the water.

I shouted to him not to be stupid but he was already on his way.

Suddenly a fierce squall filled out the sail and I struggled for the tiller. The wind was blowing the boat across the island and away from the town. I tried to turn the tiller and nearly overturned. I sat horrified while the boat sped along like a frenzied animal. I thought of lowering the sail but as soon as I let go of the tiller, the sail flapped savagely and I had to grab the tiller to steady the boat again. I cursed that bloody fool and his showing off. He would have known what to do. We were still going across the island, and I could see me being blown out to sea and dying a violent death at the jaws of a shark or something. We passed the island, the boat and I, and we were still going in the wrong direction. Then just as suddenly as it had started the wind died away. I rushed for the sail and lowered it.

I could not find him. I called for him, yelled out for him, screamed for him. I tried to turn the boat round to go back to the island, but as soon as I put up the sail the wind filled it out and took me in the opposite direction. I didn't know what to do.

You left me, Bossy. You played your games once too often.

Bossy, what happened to you?

Bossy you left me.

Bossy, what happened to you?

Bossy, I sat in that boat frightened to death that you might be in trouble but there was nothing I could do. The boat was too big for me, the water was too deep for me, and you were nowhere in sight Bossy. I called for you and all the time Bossy I was moving away from you. Bossy O Bossy, my Bossy, you wanted to make me feel a fool while you swam to land and I felt like a fool but where did you go Bossy? I did all I could with that boat but I could not turn it back to you. You would have admired its power Bossy, you would have admired its power, even while you laughed at me you would have admired its power. I tried all I could . . . What else is there to say? I turned the boat round once but I lost control and had to lower the sail. When I put it up the wind took me away from you again.

Bossy, what happened to you?

I tried all I could.

I stayed there and called out for you and called and cried out for you.

Then I thought that maybe I was just being a fool, that you were safe and well and on your way back to the town. Then I thought that maybe I would never make it back to the town myself and I was angry at what you had done Bossy and I stood up in the boat and called you names for running off and leaving me like that.

And all the time I was sailing further away from you.

And all the time I knew that I had lost you.

I called you a bastard for making me feel such pain. And all the time I knew that you had left me.

I made it back to land. I don't know how.

You missed the worst, Bossy.

That night I landed at Mbweni and walked the three miles to town. I did not get past the golf course. I was beaten by men with sticks and stones and they told me the day had come. They beat me and said this was the day when all Arabs would get theirs. They beat me and the blood was pouring off my face and I don't remember. I came to on the beach by the golf course. There was the sound of gunfire in the air. I did not recognise it at first, it sounded like children playing with pop guns. I struggled along the beach bleeding and weak. I got as far as Shangani before I was stopped by some wild men with pangas and guns and they said I was askari from the barracks and they wanted to shoot me. They said they had overrun the barracks and the Prime Minister had surrendered and they had beaten the fuck out of him. They said the day had come and all the Arabs would get theirs. They said the sultan had already run away to the ship off the harbour and if they were to get hold of him they would whip his kikoi off and fuck his arse before stuffing it full of dynamite. They said I deserved to die for being an Arab, they said anybody who was no good must be an Arab. They said where did you get those cuts if you weren't at the barracks? They said it was all over and what was I shaking like that about. They said this fellow is a weakling; shall we fuck him first before we put a bullet in him? They said we have not time and they said kill him now before the others get to the rich houses. They said if we don't hurry all the best stuff will be gone and all the good women will be ruined. They said don't waste a bullet on him, here let me show him my steel. Here they said, hold this . . . but I was too tired and weak and they beat me and urinated on me and left me lying senseless on the beach.

You missed the worst, Bossy.

The Spider's Web

Leonard Kibera

Inside the coffin, his body had become rigid. He tried to turn and only felt the prick of the nail. It had been hammered carelessly through the lid, just falling short of his shoulder. There was no pain but he felt irretrievable and alone, hemmed within the mean, stuffy box, knowing that outside was air. *As dust to dust* . . . the pious preacher intoned out there, not without an edge of triumph. *This suicide, brethren . . .!* They had no right, these people had no right at all. They sang so mournfully over him, almost as if it would disappoint them to see him come back. But he would jump out yet, he would send the rusty nails flying back at them and teach that cheap-jack of an undertaker how to convert old trunks. He was not a third class citizen. *Let me out!* But he could not find the energy to cry out or even turn a little from the nail on his shoulder, as the people out there hastened to cash in another tune, for the padre might at any moment cry *Amen!* and commit the flesh deep into the belly of the earth whence it came. Somebody was weeping righteously in between the pauses. He thought it was Mrs Njogu. Then in the dead silence that followed he was being posted into the hole and felt himself burning up already as his mean little trunk creaked at the joints and nudged its darkness in on him like a load of sins. *Careful, careful, he is not a heap of rubbish. . .* That was Mr Njogu. Down, slowly down, the careless rope issued in snappy mean measures like a spider's web and knocked his little trunk against the sides to warn the loud gates that he was coming to whoever would receive him. It caved in slowly, the earth, he could feel, and for the first time he felt important. He seemed to matter now, as all eyes no doubt narrowed into the dark hole at this moment, with everybody hissing *poor soul; gently, gently.* Then *snap!* The rope gave way—one portion of the dangling thing preferring to recoil into the tight-fisted hands out there—and he felt shot towards the bottom head-downwards, exploding into the gates of hell with a loud, unceremonious *Bang!*

Ngotho woke up with a jump. He mopped the sweat on the tail of his sheet. This kind of thing would bring him no good. Before, he had been dreaming of beer parties or women or fights with bees as he tried to smoke them out for honey. Now, lately, it seemed that when he wasn't being smoked out of this city where he so very much belonged and yet never belonged, he was either pleading his case at the White Gates or being condemned to hell in cheap coffins. *This kind of thing just isn't healthy. . .*

But he was in top form. He flung the blanket away. He bent his arms at the elbow for exercise. He shot them up and held them there like a surrender. *No that will not do.* He bent them again and pressed his fingers on his shoulders. They gathered strength, knitting into a ball so that his knuckles sharpened. Then he shot a dangerous fist to the left and held it there, tightly, not yielding a step, until he felt all stiff and blood pumped at his forehead. Dizziness overpowered him and his hand fell dead on the bed. Then a spasm uncoiled his right which came heavily on the wall and, pained, cowered. Was he still a stranger to the small dimensions of his only room even after eight years?

But it wasn't the first time anyhow. So, undaunted, he sprang twice on the bed for more exercise. Avoiding the spring that had fetched his thigh yesterday morning between the bulges in the old mattress, he hummed *Africa nchi yetu* and shot his leg down the bed. Swa—ah! That would be three shillings for another sheet through the back doors of the Koya Mosque. Ngotho dragged himself out of bed.

It was a beautiful Sunday morning. He had nothing to worry about so long as he did not make the mistake of going to church. Churches depressed him. But that dream still bothered him. (*At least they could have used a less precipitate rope*). And those nails, didn't he have enough things pricking him since Mrs Knight gave him a five-pound handshake saying Meet you in England and Mrs Njogu came buzzing in as his new memsahib borrowing two shillings from him?

Ngotho folded his arms at his chest and yawned. He took his

moustache thoughtfully between his fingers and curled it sharp like horns. At least she could have returned it. It was not as if the cost of living had risen the way employers took things for granted these days. He stood at the door of the two-room house which he shared with the other servant who, unlike him, didn't cook for memsahib. Instead, Kago went on errands, trimmed the grass and swept the compound, taking care to trace well the dog's mess for the night. Already Ngotho could see the early riser as good as sniffing and scanning the compound after the erratic manner of Wambui last night. (Wambui was the brown Alsatian dragged from the village and surprised into civilisation, a dog-collar and tinned bones by Mrs Njogu. A friend of hers, Elsie Bloom, kept one and they took their bitches for a walk together.) Ngotho cleared his throat.

'Hei, Kago!'

Kago who was getting frostbite rubbed his thumb between the toes and turned round.

'How is the dog's breakfast?'

'Nyukwa!'

Nogotho laughed.

'You don't have to insult my mother,' he said. 'Tinned bones for Wambui and cornflakes for memsahib are the same thing. We both hang if we don't get them.'

Kago leant on his broom, scratched the top of his head dull-wittedly, and at last saw that Ngotho had a point there.

He was a good soul, Kago was, and subservient as a child. There was no doubt about his ready aggressiveness where men of his class were concerned it was true, but when it came to Mrs Njogu he wound tail between his legs and stammered. This morning he was feeling at peace with the world.

'Perhaps you are right,' he said, to Ngotho. Then diving his thumb between the toes he asked if there was a small thing going on that afternoon—like a beer party.

'The Queen!'

At the mention of the name, Kago forgot everything about drinking, swerved round and felt a thousand confused things beat into his head simultaneously. Should he go on sweeping and sniffing or should he get the Bob's Tinned? Should he un-tin the Bob's Tinned or should he run for the Sunday paper? Mrs Njogu, alias queen, wasn't she more likely to want Wambui brushed behind the ear? Or was she now coming to ask him why the rope lay at the door while Wambui ran about untied?

With his bottom towards memsahib's door, Kago assumed a busy pose and peeped through his legs. But memsahib wasn't bothered about him. At least not yet. She stood at the door legs askew and admonished Ngotho about the corn-flakes.

Kago breathed a sigh of relief and took a wild sweep at the broom. He saw Ngotho back against the wall of their servant's-quarters and suppressed a laugh. After taking a torrent of English words, Ngotho seemed to tread carefully the fifty violent paces between the two doors, the irreconcilable gap between the classes. As he approached Mrs Njogu, he seemed to sweep a tactful curve off the path, as if to move up the wall first and then try to back in slowly towards the master's door and hope memsahib would make way. For her part, the queen flapped her wings and spread herself luxuriously, as good as saying, You will have to kneel and dive in through my legs. Then she stuck out her tongue twice, heaved her breasts, spat milk and honey onto the path, and disappeared into the hive. Ngotho followed her.

Kago scratched his big toe and sat down to laugh.

Breakfast for memsahib was over. Ngotho came out of the house to cut out the painful corn in his toe with the kitchen knife. He could take the risk and it pleased him. But he had to move to the other end of the wall. Mr Njogu was flushing the toilet and he might chance to open the small blurred window and see the otherwise clean kitchen knife glittering in the sun on dirty toe nails.

Breakfast. Couldn't memsahib trust him with the sugar or milk even after four years? Must she buzz around him as he measured breakfast-for-two? He had nothing against corn flakes. In fact ever since she became suspicious, he had found himself eating more of her meals whenever she was not in sight, also taking some sugar in his breast pocket. But he had come to hate himself for it and felt it was a coward's way out. Still, what was he to do? Mrs Njogu had become more and more of a stranger and he had even caught himself looking at her from an angle where formerly he had stared her straight in the face. He had wanted to talk to her, to assure her that he was still her trusted servant, but everything had become more entangled and sensitive. She would only say he was criticising, and if he wasn't happy what was he waiting for? But if he left, where was he to go? Unemployment had turned loose upon the country as it had never done before. Housewives around would receive the news of his impertinence blown high and wide over Mrs Njogu's telephone before he approached them for a job, and set their dogs on him.

Ngotho scratched at his grey hair and knew that respect for age had completely bereft his people. Was this the girl he once knew as Lois back in his home village? She had even been friends with his own daughter. A shy, young thing with pimples and thin legs. Lois had taught at the village school and was everybody's good example. She preferred to wear cheap skirts than see her aging parents starve for lack of money.

'Be like Lois,' mothers warned their daughters and even spanked them to press the point. What they meant in fact was that their daughters should, like Lois, stay unmarried longer and not simply run off with some young man in a neat tie who refused to pay the dowry. Matters soon became worse for such girls when suddenly Lois became heroine of the village. She went to jail.

It was a General Knowledge class. Lois put the problem word squarely on the blackboard. The lady supervisor who went round the schools stood squarely at the other end, looking down the class. Lois swung her stick up and down the class and said,

'What is the Commonwealth, children? Don't be shy, what does this word mean?'

The girls chewed their thumbs.

'Come on! All right. We shall start from the *beginning*. Who rules England?'

Slowly, the girls turned their heads round and faced the white supervisor. Elizabeth, they knew they should say. But how could Lois bring them to this? England sounded venerable enough. Must they go further now and let the white lady there at the back hear the Queen of England mispronounced, or even uttered by these tender things with the stain of last night's onions in their breath? Who would be the first? They knit their knuckles under the desks, looked into their exercise books, and one by one said they didn't know. One or two brave ones threw their heads back again, met with a strange look in the white queen's eye which spelt disaster, immediately swung their eyes onto the blackboard, and catching sight of Lois's stick, began to cry.

'It is as if you have never heard of it.' Lois was losing patience. 'All right, I'll give you another start. Last start. What is our country?'

Simultaneously, a flash of hands shot up from under the desks and thirty-four breaths of maize and onions clamoured.

'A colony!'

Slowly, the lady supervisor measured out light taps down the class and having eliminated the gap that came between master and servant, stood face to face with Lois.

The children chewed at their rubbers.

Then the white queen slapped Lois across the mouth and started for the door. But Lois caught her by the hair, slapped her back once, twice, and spat into her face. Then she gave her a football kick and swept her out with a right.

When at last Lois looked back into the class, she only saw torn exercise books flung on the floor. Thirty-four pairs of legs had fled home through the window, partly to be comforted from the queen's government which was certain to come, and partly to spread the formidable news of their new queen and heroine.

Queen, she certainly was, Ngotho thought as he sat by the wall and backed against it. Cornflakes in bed; expensive skirts; cigarettes. Was this her? Mr Njogu had come straight from the University College in time to secure a shining job occupied for years by a mzungu. Then a neat car was seen to park by Lois's house. In due course these visits became more frequent and alarming, but no villager was surprised when eventually Njogu succeeded in dragging Lois away from decent society. He said paying the dowry was for people in the mountains.

As luck would have it for Ngotho, Mr and Mrs Knight left and Mr and Mrs Njogu came to occupy the house. He was glad to cook and wash a black man's towels for a change. And, for a short time at any rate, he was indeed happy. Everybody had sworn that they were going to build something together, something challenging and responsible, something that would make a black man respectable in his own country. He had been willing to serve, to keep up the fire that had eventually smoked out the white man. From now on there would be no more revenge, and no more exploitation. Beyond this, he didn't expect much for himself; he knew that there would always be masters and servants.

Ngotho scratched himself between the legs and sunk against the wall. He stared at the spider that slowly built its web meticulously under the verandah roof. He threw a light stone at it and only alerted the spider.

Had his heart not throbbed with thousands of others that day as each time he closed his eyes he saw a vision of something exciting, a legacy of responsibilities that demanded a warrior's spirit? Had he not prayed for oneness deep from the heart? But it seemed to him now that a common goal had been lost sight of and he lamented it. He could not help but feel that the warriors had laid down their arrows and had parted different ways to fend for themselves. And as he thought of their households, he saw only the image of Lois who he dared call nothing but memsahib now. She swam big and muscular in his mind.

Ngotho wondered whether this was the compound he used to know. Was this part connecting master and servant the one that had been so straight during Mrs Knight?

Certainly he would never want her back. He had been kicked several times by Mr Knight and had felt what it was like to be hit with a frying pan by Mrs Knight as she reminded him to be grateful. But it had all been so direct, no ceremonies: they didn't like his broad nose. They said so. They thought there were rats under his bed. There were. They teased that he hated everything white and yet his hair was going white on his head like snow, a cool white protector while below the black animal simmered and plotted: wouldn't he want it cut? No, he wouldn't. Occasionally, they would be impressed by a well-turned turkey or chicken and say so over talk of the white man's responsibility in Africa. If they were not in the mood they just dismissed him and told him not to forget the coffee. Ngotho knew that all this was because they were becoming uneasy and frightened, and that perhaps they had to point the gun at all black men now at a time when even the church had taken sides. But whatever the situation in the house, there was nevertheless a frankness about the black-and-white relationship where no ceremonies or apologies were necessary in a world of mutual distrust and hate. And if Mrs Knight scolded him all over the house, it was Mr Knight who seemed to eventually lock the bedroom door and come heavily on top of her and everybody else although, Ngotho thought, they were all ruled by a woman in England.

Ngotho walked heavily to the young tree planted three years ago by Mrs Njogu and wondered why he should have swept a curve off the path that morning, as memsahib filled the door. He knew it wasn't the first time he had done that. Everything had become crooked, subtle, and he had to watch his step. His monthly vernacular paper said so. He felt cornered. He gripped the young tree by the scruff of the neck and shook it furiously. What the hell was wrong with some men anyway? Had Mr Njogu become a male weakling in a fat queen bee's hive, slowly being milked dry and sapless, dying? Where was the old warrior who at the end of the battle would go home to his wife and make her moan under his heavy sweat? All he could see now as he shook the tree was a line of neat houses. There, the warriors had come to their battle's end and parted, to forget other warriors and to be mothered to sleep without even knowing it, meeting only occasionally to drink beer and sing traditional songs. And where previously the bow and arrow lay by the bed-post, Ngotho now only saw a conspiracy of round tablets while a *Handbook of Novel Techniques* lay by the pillow.

He had tried to understand. But as he looked at their pregnant wives he could foresee nothing but a new generation of innocent snobs, who would be chauffeured off to school in neat caps hooded over their eyes so as to obstruct vision. There they would learn that the other side of the city was dirty. Ngotho spat right under the tree. Once or twice he would have liked to kick Mr Njogu. He looked all so sensibly handsome and clean as he buzzed after his wife on a broken wing and—a spot of jam on his tie—said he wanted the key to the car.

He had also become very sensitive and self-conscious.

Ngotho couldn't complain a little or even make a joke about the taxes without somebody detecting a subtler intention behind the smile, where the servant was supposed to be on a full-scale plotting. And there was behind the master and the queen now a bigger design, a kind of pattern meticulously fenced above the hive; a subtle web, at the centre of which lurked the spider which protected, watched and jailed. Ngotho knew only too well that the web had been slowly, quietly in the making and a pebble thrown at it would at best alert and fall back impotent on the ground.

He took a look at the other end of the compound. Kago had fallen asleep, while Wambui ran about untied, the rope still lying at the door. Kago wore an indifferent grin. Ngotho felt overpowered, trapped, alone. He spat in Kago's direction and plucked a twig off one of the branches on the tree. The tree began to bleed. He tightened his grip and shed the reluctant leaves down. Just what had gone wrong with God?

The old one had faithfully done his job when that fig tree near Ngotho's village withered away as predicted by the tribal seer. It had been the local news and lately, it was rumoured, some businessman would honour the old god by erecting a hotel on the spot. Ngotho hardly believed in any god at all. The one lived in corrupted blood, the other in pulpits of hypocrisy. But at least while they kept neat themselves they could have honoured the old in a cleaner way. How could this new saviour part the warriors different ways into isolated compartments, to flush their uneasy hotel toilets all over the old one?

Ngotho passed a reverent hand over his wrinkled forehead and up his white hair. He plucked another twig off the dangerous tree. Something was droning above his ear.

'What are you doing to my tree?'

The buzzing had turned into a scream.

'I—I want to pick my teeth,' Ngotho unwrapped a row of defiant molars.

The queen flapped her wings and landed squarely on the ground. Then she was heaving heavily, staring at him out of small eyes. He tried to back away from her eyes. Beyond her, in the background, he caught sight of Mr Njogu through the bedroom window polishing his spectacles on his pyjama sleeve, trying desperately to focus—clearly—on the situation outside. A flap of the wing and Ngotho felt hit right across the mouth, by the hand that had once hit the white lady. Then the queen wobbled in midflight, settled at the door, and screamed at Mr Njogu to come out and prove he was a man.

Mr Njogu didn't like what he saw. He threw his glasses away and preferred to see things blurred.

'These women,' he muttered, and waved them away with a neat pyjama sleeve. Then he buried his head under the blanket and snored. It was ten o'clock.

Ngotho stood paralysed. He had never been hit by a woman before, outside of his mother's hut. Involuntarily, he felt his eyes snap shut and his eyelids burn red, violently, in the sun. Then out of the spider's web in his mind, policemen, magistrates and third class undertakers flew in profusion. He opened up, sweating, and the kitchen knife in his hand fell down, stabbing the base of the tree where it vibrated once, twice, and fell flat on its side, dead.

Then with a cry, he grabbed it and rushed into the house. But Mr Njogu saw him coming as the knife glittered nearer and clearer in his direction, and leapt out of bed.

Suddenly the horror of what he had done caught Ngotho. He could hear the queen at least crying hysterically into the telephone, while Mr Njogu locked himself in the toilet and began weeping. Ngotho looked at the kitchen knife in his hand. He had only succeeded in stabbing Mr Njgou in the thigh, and the knife had now turned red on him. Soon the sticky web would stretch a thread. And he would be caught as he never thought he would when first he felt glad to work for Lois.

He saw Wambui's rope still lying in a noose. Then he went into his room and locked the door.

Minutes of Glory

Ngugi wa Thiong'o

Her name was Wanjiru. But she liked better her Christian one, Beatrice. It sounded more pure and more beautiful. Not that she was ugly; but she could not be called beautiful either. Her body, dark and full fleshed, had the form, yes, but it was as if it waited to be filled by the spirit. She worked in beer-halls where sons of women came to drown their inner lives in beer cans and froth. Nobody seemed to notice her. Except, perhaps, when a proprietor or an impatient customer called out her name, Beatrice; then other customers would raise their heads briefly, a few seconds, as if to behold the bearer of such a beautiful name, but not finding anybody there, they would resume their drinking, their ribald jokes, their laughter and play with the other serving girls. She was like a wounded bird in flight: a forced landing now and then but nevertheless wobbling from place to place so that she would variously be found in Alaska, Paradise, The Modern, Thome and other beer-halls all over Limuru. Sometimes it was because an irate proprietor found she was not attracting enough customers; he would sack her without notice and without a salary. She would wobble to the next bar. But sometimes she was simply tired of nesting in one place, a daily witness of familiar scenes; girls even more decidedly ugly than she were fought over by numerous claimants at closing hours. What do they have that I don't have? she would ask herself, depressed. She longed for a bar-kingdom where she would be at least one of the rulers, where petitioners would bring their gifts of beer, frustrated smiles and often curses that hid more lust and love than hate.

She left Limuru town proper and tried the mushrooming townlets around. She worked at Ngarariga, Kamiritho, Rironi and even Tiekunu and everywhere the story was the same. Oh, yes, occasionally she would get a client; but none cared for

her as she would have liked, none really wanted her enough to
fight over her. She was always a hard-up customer's last
resort. No make-believe even, not for her that sweet pretence
that men indulged in after their fifth bottle of Tusker. The
following night or during a pay-day, the same client would
pretend not to know her; he would be trying his money-power
over girls who already had more than a fair share of admirers.

She resented this. She saw in every girl a rival and adopted a
sullen attitude. Nyagũthiĩ especially was the thorn that always
pricked her wounded flesh. Nyagũthiĩ arrogant and aloof, but
men always in her courtyard; Nyagũthiĩ fighting with men,
and to her they would bring propitiating gifts which she
accepted as of right. Nyagũthiĩ could look bored, impatient,
or downright contemptuous and still men would cling to her
as if they enjoyed being whipped with biting words, curled
lips and the indifferent eyes of a free woman. Nyagũthiĩ was
also a bird in flight, never really able to settle in one place, but
in her case it was because she hungered for change and excitement: new faces and new territories for her conquest. Beatrice
resented her very shadow. She saw in her the girl she would
have liked to be, a girl who was both totally immersed in and
yet completely above the underworld of bar violence and sex.
Wherever Beatrice went the long shadow of Nyagũthiĩ would
sooner or later follow her.

She fled Limuru for Ilmorog in Chiri District. Ilmorog had
once been a ghost village, but had been resurrected to life by
that legendary woman, Nyang'endo, to whom every pop
group had paid their tribute. It was of her that the young
dancing Muthuu and Muchun g'wa sang:

> When I left Nairobi for Ilmorog
> Never did I know
> I would bear this wonder-child mine
> Nyang'endo.

As a result, Ilmorog was always seen as a town of hope where
the weary and the down-trodden would find their rest and
fresh water. But again Nyagũthiĩ followed her.

She found that Ilmorog, despite the legend, despite the

songs and dances, was not different from Limuru. She tried various tricks. Clothes? But even here she never earned enough to buy herself glittering robes. What was seventy-five shillings a month without house allowance, posho, without salaried boy-friends? By that time, Ambi had reached Ilmorog, and Beatrice thought that this would be the answer. Had she not, in Limuru, seen girls blacker than herself transformed overnight from ugly sins into white stars by a touch of skin-lightening creams? And men would ogle them, would even talk with exaggerated pride of their newborn girl friends. Men were strange creatures, Beatrice thought in moments of searching analysis. They talked heatedly against Ambi, Butone, Firesnow, Moonsnow, wigs, straightened hair; but they always went for a girl with an Ambi-lightened skin and head covered with a wig made in imitation of European or Indian hair. Beatrice never tried to find the root cause of this black self-hatred, she simply accepted the contradiction and applied herself to Ambi with a vengeance. She had to rub out her black shame. But even Ambi she could not afford in abundance; she could only apply it to her face and her arms so that her legs and neck retained their blackness. Besides there were parts of her face she could not readily reach—behind the ears and above the eyelashes, for instance—and these were a constant source of shame and irritation for her Ambi-self.

She would always remember this Ambi period as one of her deepest humiliation before her later minutes of glory. She worked in Ilmorog Starlight Bar and Lodging. Nyagũthiĩ with her bangled hands, her huge earrings, served behind the counter. The owner was a good Christian soul who regularly went to church and paid all his dues to Harambee projects. Pot-belly. Grey hairs. Soft-spoken. A respectable family man, well known in Ilmorog. Hardworking even, for he would not leave the bar until the closing hours, or more precisely, until Nyagũthiĩ left. He had no eyes for any other girl; he hung around her, and surreptitiously brought her gifts of clothes without receiving gratitude in kind. Only the promise. Only the hope for tomorrow. Other girls he gave eighty shillings a month. Nyagũthiĩ had a room to herself. Nyagũthiĩ woke up whenever she liked to take the stock. But Beatrice and the other girls had to wake up at five or so, make tea for the lodgers, clean up the bar and wash dishes and glasses. Then they would hang around the bar and in shifts until two o'clock when they would go for a small break. At five o'clock, they had to be in again, ready for customers whom they would now serve with frothy beers and smiles until twelve o'clock or for as long as there were customers thirsty for more Tuskers and Pilsners. What often galled Beatrice, although in her case it did not matter one way or another, was the owner's insistence that the girls should sleep in Starlight. They would otherwise be late for work, he said. But what he really wanted was for the girls to use their bodies to attract more lodgers in Starlight. Most of the girls, led by Nyagūthiī defied the rule and bribed the watchman to let them out and in. They wanted to meet their regular or one-night boy-friends in places where they would be free and where they would be treated as not just barmaids. Beatrice always slept in. Her occasional one-night patrons wanted to spend the minimum. Came a night when the owner, refused by Nyagūthiī, approached her. He started by finding fault with her work; he called her names, then as suddenly he started praising her, although in a grudging almost contemptuous manner. He grabbed her, struggled with her, pot-belly, grey hairs, and everything. Beatrice felt an unusual revulsion for the man. She could not, she would not bring herself to accept that which had so recently been cast aside by Nyagūthiī. My God, she wept inside, what does Nyagūthiī have that I don't have? The man now humiliated himself before her. He implored. He promised her gifts. But she would not yield. That night she too defied the rule. She jumped through a window; she sought a bed in another bar and only came back at six. The proprietor called her in front of all the others and dismissed her. But Beatrice was rather surprised at herself.

She stayed a month without a job. She lived from room to room at the capricious mercy of the other girls. She did not have the heart to leave Ilmorog and start all over again in a new town. The wound hurt. She was tired of wandering. She stopped using Ambi. No money. She looked at herself in the mirror. She had so aged, hardly a year after she had fallen from grace. Why then was she scrupulous, she would ask herself. But somehow she had a horror of soliciting lovers or directly bartering her body for hard cash. What she wanted was decent work and a man or several men who cared for her. Perhaps she took that need for a man, for a home and for a child with her to bed. Perhaps it was this genuine need that scared off men who wanted other things from barmaids. She wept late at nights and remembered home. At such moments, her mother's village in Nyeri seemed the sweetest place on God's earth. She would invest the life of her peasant mother and father with romantic illusions of immeasurable peace and harmony. She longed to go back home to see them. But how could she go back with empty hands? In any case the place was now a distant landscape in the memory. Her life was here in the bar among this crowd of lost strangers. Fallen from grace, fallen from grace. She was part of a generation which would never again be one with the soil, the crops, the wind and the moon. Not for them that whispering in dark hedges, not for her that dance and love-making under the glare of the moon, with the hills of Tumu Tumu rising to touch the sky. She remembered that girl from her home village who, despite a life of apparent glamour being the kept mistress of one rich man after another in Limuru, had gassed herself to death. This generation was now awed by the mystery of death, just as it was callous to the mystery of life; for how many unmarried mothers had thrown their babies into latrines rather than lose that glamour? The girl's death became the subject of jokes. She had gone metric—without pains, they said. Thereafter, for a week, Beatrice thought of going metric. But she could not bring herself to do it.

She wanted love; she wanted life.

A new bar was opened in Ilmorog. Treetop Bar, Lodging and Restaurant. Why Treetop, Beatrice could not understand unless because it was a storied building: tea-shop on the ground floor and beer-shop in a room at the top. The rest were rooms for five-minute or one-night lodgers. The owner was a retired civil servant but one who still played at politics. He was enormously wealthy with business sites and enterprises in every major town in Kenya. Big shots from all over the country came to his bar. Big men in Mercedes. Big men in their Bentleys. Big men in their Jaguars and Daimlers. Big men with uniformed chauffeurs drowsing with boredom in cars waiting

outside. There were others not so big who came to pay
respects to the great. They talked politics mostly. And about
their work. Gossip was rife. Didn't you know? Indeed so and
so has been promoted. Really? And so and so has been sacked.
Embezzlement of public funds. So foolish you know. Not
clever about it at all. They argued, they quarrelled, sometimes
they fought it out with fists, especially during the elections
campaign. The only point on which they were all agreed was
that the Luo community was the root cause of all the trouble in
Kenya; that intellectuals and University students were living
in an ivory tower of privilege and arrogance; that Kiambu had
more than a lion's share of developments; that men from Nyeri
and Muranga had acquired all the big business in Nairobi and
were even encroaching on Chiri District; that African workers,
especially those on the farms, were lazy and jealous of 'us'
who had sweated ourselves to sudden prosperity. Otherwise
each would hymn his own praises or return compliments.
Occasionally in moments of drunken ebullience and self-
praise, one would order two rounds of beer for each man
present in the bar. Even the poor from Ilmorog would come to
Treetop to dine at the gates of the nouveaux riches.

Here Beatrice got a job as a sweeper and bedmaker. Here for
a few weeks she felt closer to greatness. Now she made beds
for men she had previously known as names. She watched
how even the poor tried to drink and act big in front of the big.
But soon fate caught up with her. Girls flocked to Treetop from
other bars. Girls she had known at Limuru, girls she had
known at Ilmorog. And most had attached themselves to one
or several big men, often playing a hide-and-not-to-be found
game with their numerous lovers. And Nyagũthiĩ was there
behind the counter, with the eyes of the rich and the poor fixed
on her. And she, with her big eyes, bangled hands and
earrings maintained the same air of bored indifference. Beatrice as a sweeper and bedmaker became even more invisible.
Girls who had fallen into good fortune looked down upon her.

She fought life with dreams. In between putting clean sheets
on beds that had just witnessed a five-minute struggle that
ended in a half-strangled cry and a pool, she would stand by
the window and watch the cars and the chauffeurs, so that
soon she knew all the owners by the number plates of their

cars and the uniforms of their chauffeurs. She dreamt of lovers
who would come for her in sleek Mercedes sports cars made
for two. She saw herself linking hands with such a lover,
walking in the streets of Nairobi and Mombasa, tapping the
ground with high heels, quick, quick short steps. And suddenly she would stop in front of a display glass window, exclaim-
ing at the same time, Oh darling, won't you buy me those. . . ?
Those what? he would ask, affecting anger. Those stockings,
darling. It was as an owner of several stockings, ladderless and
holeless, that she thought of her well-being. Never again
would she mend torn things. Never, never, never. Do you
understand? Never. She was next the proud owner of different
coloured wigs, blonde wigs, brunette wigs, redhead wigs,
Afro wigs, wigs, wigs, all the wigs in the world. Only then
would the whole earth sing hallelujah to the one Beatrice. At
such moments, she would feel exalted, lifted out of her murky
self, no longer a floor sweeper and bedmaker for a five-minute
instant love, but Beatrice, descendant of Wangu Makeri who
made men tremble with desire at her naked body bathed in
moonlight, daughter of Nyang'endo, the founder of modern
Ilmorog, of whom they often sang that she had worked several
lovers into impotence.

Then she noticed him and he was the opposite of the lover of
her dreams. He came one Saturday afternoon driving a big
five-ton lorry. He carefully parked it beside the Benzes, the
Jaguars and the Daimlers, not as a lorry, but as one of those
sleek cream-bodied frames, so proud of it he seemed to be. He
dressed in a baggy grey suit over which he wore a heavy khaki
military overcoat. He removed the overcoat, folded it with
care, and put it in the front seat. He locked all the doors,
dusted himself a little, then walked round the lorry as if
inspecting it for damage. A few steps before he entered
Treetop, he turned round for a final glance at his lorry dwarf-
ing the other things. At Treetops he sat in a corner and, with a
rather loud defiant voice, ordered a Kenya one. He drank it
with relish, looking around at the same time for a face he might
recognize. He indeed did recognize one of the big ones and he
immediately ordered for him a quarter bottle of Vat 69. This
was accepted with a bare nod of the head and a patronising
smile; but when he tried to follow his generosity with a

conversation, he was firmly ignored. He froze, sank into his Muratina. But only for a time. He tried again: he was met with frowning faces. More pathetic were his attempts to join in jokes; he would laugh rather too loudly, which would make the big ones stop, leaving him in the air alone. Later in the evening he stood up, counted several crisp hundred shilling notes and handed them to Nyagũthiĩ behind the counter ostensibly for safekeeping. People whispered; murmured; a few laughed, rather derisively, though they were rather impressed. But this act did not win him immediate recognition. He staggered towards room no. 7 which he had hired. Beatrice brought him the keys. He glanced at her, briefly, then lost all interest.

Thereafter he came every Saturday. At five when most of the big shots were already seated. He repeated the same ritual, except the money act, and always met with defeat. He nearly always sat in the same corner and always rented room 7. Beatrice grew to anticipate his visits and, without being conscious of it, kept the room ready for him. Often after he had been badly humiliated by the big company, he would detain Beatrice and talk to her, or rather he talked to himself in her presence. For him, it had been a life of struggles. He had never been to school although getting an education had been his ambition. He never had a chance. His father was a squatter in the European settled area in the Rift Valley. That meant a lot in those colonial days. It meant among other things a man and his children were doomed to a future of sweat and toil for the white devils and their children. He had joined the freedom struggle and like the others had been sent to detention. He came from detention the same as his mother had brought him to this world. Nothing. With independence he found he did not possess the kind of education which would have placed him in one of the vacancies at the top. He started as a charcoal burner, then a butcher, gradually working his own way to become a big transporter of vegetables and potatoes from the Rift Valley and Chiri districts to Nairobi. He was proud of his achievement. But he resented that others, who had climbed to their present wealth through loans and a subsidized education, would not recognize his like. He would rumble on like this, dwelling on education he would never have, and talking of better chances for his children. Then he would carefully count the money, put it under the pillow, and then dismiss Beatrice. Occasionally he would buy her a beer but he was clearly suspicious of women whom he saw as money-eaters of men. He had not yet married.

One night he slept with her. In the morning he scratched for a twenty shilling note and gave it to her. She accepted the money with an odd feeling of guilt. He did this for several weeks. She did not mind the money. It was useful. But he paid for her body as he would pay for a bag of potatoes or a sack of cabbages. With the one pound, he had paid for her services as a listener, a vessel of his complaints against those above, and as a one-night receptacle of his man's burden. She was becoming bored with his ego, with his stories that never varied in content, but somehow, in him, deep inside, she felt that something had been there, a fire, a seed, a flower which was being smothered. In him she saw a fellow victim and looked forward to his visits. She too longed to talk to someone. She too longed to confide in a human being who would understand.

And she did it one Saturday night, suddenly interrupting the story of his difficult climb to the top. She did not know why she did it. Maybe it was the rain outside. It was softly drumming the corrugated iron sheets, bringing with the drumming a warm and drowsy indifference. He would listen. He had to listen. She came from Karatina in Nyeri. Her two brothers had been gunned down by the British soldiers. Another one had died in detention. She was, so to speak, an only child. Her parents were poor. But they worked hard on their bare strip of land and managed to pay her fees in primary school. For the first six years she had worked hard. In the seventh year, she must have relaxed a little. She did not pass with a good grade. Of course she knew many with similar grades who had been called to good government secondary schools. She knew a few others with lesser grades who had gone to very top schools on the strength of their connections. But she was not called to any high school with reasonable fees. Her parents could not afford fees in a Harambee school. And she would not hear of repeating standard seven. She stayed at home with her parents. Occasionally she would help them in the shamba and with

house chores. But imagine: for the past six years she had led a
life with a different rhythm from that of her parents. Life in the
village was dull. She would often go to Karatina and to Nyeri
in search of work. In every office, they would ask her the same
questions: what work do you want? What do you know? Can
you type? Can you take shorthand? She was desperate. It was
in Nyeri, drinking Fanta in a shop, tears in her eyes, that she
met a young man in a dark suit and sun-glasses. He saw her
plight and talked to her. He came from Nairobi. Looking for
work? That's easy; in a big city there would be no difficulty
with jobs. He would certainly help. Transport? He had a
car—a cream-white Peugeot. Heaven. It was a beautiful ride,
with the promise of dawn. Nairobi. He drove her to Terrace
Bar. They drank beer and talked about Nairobi. Through the
window she could see the neon-lit city and knew that here was
hope. That night she gave herself to him, with the promise of
dawn making her feel light and gay. She had a very deep sleep.
When she woke in the morning, the man in the cream-white
Peugeot was not there. She never saw him again. That's how
she had started the life of a barmaid. And for one and a half
years now she had not been once to see her parents. Beatrice
started weeping. Huge sobs of self-pity. Her humiliation and
constant flight were fresh in her mind. She had never been
able to take to bar culture, she always thought that something
better would come her way. But she was trapped, it was the
only life she now knew, although she had never really learnt
all its laws and norms. Again she heaved out and in, tears
tossing out with every sob. Then suddenly she froze. Her
sobbing was arrested in the air. The man had long covered
himself. His snores were huge and unmistakable.

She felt a strange hollowness. Then a bile of bitterness spilt
inside her. She wanted to cry at her new failure. She had met
several men who had treated her cruelly, who had laughed at
her scruples, at what they thought was an ill-disguised
attempt at innocence. She had accepted. But not this, Lord,
not this. Was this man not a fellow victim? Had he not,
Saturday after Saturday, unburdened himself to her? He had
paid for her human services; he had paid away his responsibility with his bottle of Tuskers and hard cash in the morning.
Her innermost turmoil had been his lullaby. And suddenly

something in her snapped. All the anger of a year and a half, all the bitterness against her humiliation were now directed at this man.

What she did later had the mechanical precision of an experienced hand.

She touched his eyes. He was sound asleep. She raised his head. She let it fall. Her tearless eyes were now cold and set. She removed the pillow from under him. She rummaged through it. She took out his money. She counted five crisp pink notes. She put the money inside her brassiere.

She went out of room no. 7. Outside it was still raining. She did not want to go to her usual place. She could not now stand the tiny cupboard room or the superior chatter of her roommate. She walked through mud and rain. She found herself walking towards Nyagŭthiĩ's room. She knocked at the door. At first she had no response. Then she heard Nyagŭthiĩ's sleepy voice above the drumming rain.

'Who is that?'

'It is me. Please open.'

'Who?'

'Beatrice.'

'At this hour of the night?'

'Please.'

Lights were put on. Bolts unfastened. The door opened. Beatrice stepped inside. She and Nyagŭthiĩ stood there face to face. Nyagŭthiĩ was in a see-through nightdress: on her shoulders she had a green pullover.

'Beatrice, is there anything wrong?' She at last asked, a note of concern in her voice.

'Can I rest here for a while? I am tired. And I want to talk to you.' Beatrice's voice carried assurance and power.

'But what has happened?'

'I only want to ask you a question, Nyagŭthiĩ'

They were still standing. Then, without a word, they both sat on the bed.

'Why did you leave home, Nyagŭthiĩ?' Beatrice asked. Another silent moment. Nyagŭthiĩ seemed to be thinking about the question. Beatrice waited. Nyagŭthiĩ's voice when at last it came was slightly tremulous, unsteady.

'It is a long story, Beatrice. My father and mother were fairly wealthy. They were also good Christians. We lived under regulations. You must never walk with the heathen. You must not attend their pagan customs—dances and circumcision rites, for instance. There were rules about what, how and when to eat. You must even walk like a Christian lady. You must never be seen with boys. Rules, rules all the way. One day instead of returning home from school, I and another girl from a similar home ran away to Eastleigh. I have never been home once this last four years. That's all.'

Another silence. Then they looked at one another in mutual recognition.

'One more question, Nyagũthiĩ. You need not answer it. But I have always thought that you hated me, you despised me.'

'No, no, Beatrice, I have never hated you. I have never hated anybody. It is just that nothing interests me. Even men do not move me now. Yet I want, I need instant excitement. I need the attention of those false flattering eyes to make me feel myself, myself. But you, you seemed above all this—somehow you had something inside you that I did not have.'

Beatrice tried to hold her tears with difficulty.

Early the next day, she boarded a bus bound for Nairobi. She walked down Bazaar Street looking at the shops. Then down Government Road, right into Kenyatta Avenue, and Kimathi Street. She went into a shop near Hussein Suleman's Street and bought several stockings. She put on a pair. She next bought herself a new dress. Again she changed into it. In a Bata Shoeshop, she bought high heeled shoes, put them on and discarded her old flat ones. On to an Akamba kiosk, and she fitted herself with earrings. She went to a mirror and looked at her new self. Suddenly she felt enormous hunger as if she had been hungry all her life. She hesitated in front of Moti Mahal. Then she walked on, eventually entering Fransae. There was a glint in her eyes that made men's eyes turn to her. This thrilled her. She chose a table in a corner and ordered Indian curry. A man left his table and joined her. She looked at him. Her eyes were merry. He was dressed in a dark suit and his eyes spoke of lust. He bought her a drink. He tried to engage her in conversation. But she ate in silence. He put his hand under the table and felt her knees. She let him do it. The hand went up and up her thigh. Then suddenly she left her unfinished food and her untouched drink and walked out. She felt good. He followed her. She knew this without once turning her eyes. He walked beside her for a few yards. She smiled at herself but did not look at him. He lost his confidence. She left him standing sheepishly looking at a glass window outside Gino's. In the bus back to Ilmorog, men gave her seats. She accepted this as of right. At Treetops bar she went straight to the counter. The usual crowd of big men were there. Their conversations stopped for a few seconds at her entry. Their lascivious eyes were turned to her. The girls stared at her. Even Nyagũthiĩ could not maintain her bored indifference. Beatrice bought them drinks. The manager came to her, rather unsure. He tried a conversation. Why had she left work? Where had she been? Would she like to work in the bar, helping Nyagũthiĩ behind the counter? Now and then? A barmaid brought her a note. A certain big shot wanted to know if she would join their table. More notes came from different big quarters with the one question; would she be free tonight? A trip to Nairobi even. She did not leave her place at the counter. But she accepted their drinks as of right. She felt a new power, confidence even.

She took out a shilling, put it in the slot and the juke box boomed with the voice of Robinson Mwangi singing *Hũnyũ wa Mashambani*. He sang of those despised girls who worked on farms and contrasted them with urban girls. Then she played a Kamaru and a D.K. Men wanted to dance with her. She ignored them, but enjoyed their flutter around her. She twisted her hips to the sound of yet another D.K. Her body was free. She was free. She sucked in the excitement and tension in the air.

Then suddenly at around six, the man with the five-ton lorry stormed into the bar. This time he had on his military overcoat. Behind him was a policeman. He looked around. Everybody's eyes were raised to him. But Beatrice went on swaying her hips. At first he could not recognize Beatrice in the girl celebrating her few minutes of glory by the juke box. Then he shouted in triumph. 'That is the girl! Thief! Thief!'

People melted back to their seats. The policeman went and handcuffed her. She did not resist. Only at the door she turned her head and spat. Then she went out followed by the policeman.

In the bar the stunned silence broke into hilarious laughter when someone made a joke about sweetened robbery without violence. They discussed her. Some said she should have been beaten. Others talked contemptuously about 'these bar girls'. Yet others talked with a concern noticeable in unbelieving shakes of their heads about the rising rate of crime. Shouldn't the Hanging Bill be extended to all thefts of property? And without anybody being aware of it the man with the five-ton lorry had become a hero. They now surrounded him with questions and demanded the whole story. Some even bought him drinks. More remarkable, they listened, their attentive silence punctuated by appreciative laughter. The averted threat to property had temporarily knit them into one family. And the man, accepted for the first time, told the story with relish.

But behind the counter Nyagŭthiĭ wept.

NORTHERN AFRICA

An Incident in the Ghobashi Household

Alifa Rifaat
translated by Denys Johnson-Davies

Zeinat woke to the strident call of the red cockerel from the rooftop above where she was sleeping. The Ghobashi house stood on the outskirts of the village and in front of it the fields stretched out to the river and the railway track.

The call of the red cockerel released answering calls from neighbouring rooftops. Then they were silenced by the voice of the muezzin from the lofty minaret among the mulberry trees calling: 'Prayer is better than sleep.'

She stretched out her arm to the pile of children sleeping alongside her and tucked the end of the old rag-woven kilim round their bodies, then shook her eldest daughter's shoulder.

'It's morning, another of the Lord's mornings. Get up, Ni'ma—today's market day.'

Ni'ma rolled onto her back and lazily stretched herself. Like someone alerted by the sudden slap of a gust of wind, Zeinat stared down at the body spread out before her. Ni'ma sat up and pulled her djellaba over her thighs, rubbing at her sleep-heavy eyes in the rounded face with the prominent cheekbones.

'Are you going to be able to carry the grain to the market, daughter, or will it be too heavy for you?'

'Of course, mother. After all, who else is there to go?'

Zeinat rose to her feet and went out with sluggish steps to the courtyard, where she made her ablutions. Having finished the ritual prayer, she remained in the seated position as she counted off on her fingers her glorifications of Allah. Sensing that Ni'ma was standing behind her, she turned round to her:

'What are you standing there for? Why don't you go off and get the tea ready?'

Zeinat walked towards the corner where Ghobashi had stored the maize crop in sacks; he had left them as a provision for them after he had taken his air ticket from the office that had found him work in Libya and which would be bringing him back in a year's time.

'May the Lord keep you safe while you're away, Ghobashi,' she muttered.

Squatting in front of a sack, the grain measure between her thighs, she scooped up the grain with both hands till the measure was full, then poured it into a basket. Coughing, she waved away the dust that rose up into her face, then returned to her work.

The girl went to the large clay jar, removed the wooden covering and dipped the mug into it and sprinkled water on her face; she wetted the tips of her fingers and parted her plaits, then tied her handkerchief over her head. She turned to her mother:

'Isn't that enough, mother? What do we want the money for?'

Zeinat struck her knees with the palms of her hands and tossed her head back.

'Don't we have to pay off Hamdan's wage?—or was he cultivating the beans for us for nothing, just for the fun of hard work?'

Ni'ma turned away and brought the stove from the window shelf, arranging the dried corn-cobs in a pyramid and lighting them. She put it alongside her mother, then filled the teapot with water from the jar and thrust it into the embers. She squatted down and the two sat in silence. Suddenly Zeinat said:

'Since when has the buffalo been with young?'

'From after my father went away.'

'That's to say, right after the Great Feast, daughter?'

Ni'ma nodded her head in assent, then lowered it and began drawing lines in the dust.

'Why don't you go off and see how many eggs have been laid while the tea's getting ready.'

Zeinat gazed into the glow of the embers. She had a sense of peace as she stared into the dancing flames. Ghobashi had gone and left the whole load on her shoulders: the children, the two kirats of land and the buffalo. 'Take care of Ni'ma,' he had said the night before he left. 'The girl's body has ripened.' He had then spread out his palms and said: 'O Lord, for the sake of the Prophet's honour, let me bring back with me a marriage dress for her of pure silk.' She had said to him: 'May your words go straight from your lips to Heaven's gate, Ghobashi.' He wouldn't be returning before the following Great Feast. What would happen when he returned and found out the state of affairs? She put her head between the palms of her hands and leaned over the fire, blowing away the ashes. 'How strange,' she thought, 'are the girls of today! The cunning little thing was hanging out her towels at the time of her period every month just as though nothing had happened, and here she is in her fourth month and there's nothing showing.'

Ni'ma returned and untied the cloth from round the eggs, put two of them in the fire and the rest in a dish. She then brought two glasses and the tin of sugar and sat down next to her mother, who was still immersed in her thoughts.

'Didn't you try to find some way out?'

Ni'ma hunched her shoulders in a gesture of helplessness.

'Your father's been gone four months. Isn't there still time?'

'What's the use? If only the Lord were to spare you the trouble of me. Wouldn't it be for the best, mother, if my foot were to slip as I was filling the water jar from the canal and we'd be done with it?'

Zeinat struck herself on the breast and drew her daughter to her.

'Don't say such a wicked thing. Don't listen to such promptings of the Devil. Calm down and let's find some solution before your father returns.'

Zeinat poured out the tea. In silence she took quick sips at it, then put the glass in front of her and shelled the egg and bit into it. Ni'ma sat watching her, her fingers held round the hot glass. From outside came the raised voices of women discussing the prospects at the day's market, while men exchanged greetings as they made their way to the fields. Amidst the voices could be heard Hamdan's laughter as he led the buffalo to the two kirats of land surrounding the house.

'His account is with Allah,' muttered Zeinat. 'He's fine and doesn't have a worry in the world.'

Ni'ma got up and began winding round the end of her headcloth so as to form a pad on her head. Zeinat turned round and saw her preparing herself to go off to the market. She pulled her by her djellaba and the young girl sat down again. At this moment they heard a knocking at the door and the voice of their neighbour, Umm al-Khair, calling:

'Good health to you, folk. Isn't Ni'ma coming with me to market as usual, Auntie Zeinat? Or isn't she up yet?'

'Sister, she's just going off to stay with our relatives.'

'May Allah bring her back safely.'

Ni'ma looked at her mother enquiringly, while Zeinat placed her finger to her mouth. When the sound of Umm al-Khair's footsteps died away, Ni'ma whispered:

'What are you intending to do, mother? What relatives are you talking about?'

Zeinat got up and rummaged in her clothes box and took out a handkerchief tied round some money, also old clothes. She placed the handkerchief in Ni'ma's palm and closed her fingers over it.

'Take it—they're my life savings.'

Ni'ma remained silent as her mother went on:

'Get together your clothes and go straight away to the station and take a ticket to Cairo. Cairo's a big place, daughter, where you'll find protection and a way to make a living till Allah brings you safely to your time. Then bring it back with you at dead of night without anyone seeing you or hearing you.'

Zeinat raised the end of her djellaba and put it between her teeth. Taking hold of the old clothes, she began winding them round her waist. Then she let fall the djellaba. Ni'ma regarded her in astonishment:

'And what will we say to my father?'

'It's not time for talking. Before you go off to the station, help me with the basket so that I can go to the market for people to see me like this. Isn't it better, when he returns, for your father to find himself with a legitimate son than an illegitimate grandson?'

A Handful of Dates

Tayeb Salih
translated by Denys Johnson-Davies

I must have been very young at the time. While I don't remember exactly how old I was, I do remember that when people saw me with my grandfather they would pat me on the head and give my cheek a pinch—things they didn't do to my grandfather. The strange thing was that I never used to go out with my father, rather it was my grandfather who would take me with him wherever he went, except for the mornings when I would go to the mosque to learn the Koran. The mosque, the river and the fields—these were the landmarks in our life. While most of the children of my age grumbled at having to go to the mosque to learn the Koran, I used to love it. The reason was, no doubt, that I was quick at learning by heart and the Sheikh always asked me to stand up and recite the *Chapter of the Merciful* whenever we had visitors, who would pat me on my head and cheek just as people did when they saw me with my grandfather.

Yes, I used to love the mosque, and I loved the river too. Directly we finished our Koran reading in the morning I would throw down my wooden slate and dart off, quick as a genie, to my mother, hurriedly swallow down my breakfast, and run off for a plunge in the river. When tired of swimming about I would sit on the bank and gaze at the strip of water that wound away eastwards and hid behind a thick wood of acacia trees. I loved to give rein to my imagination and picture to myself a tribe of giants living behind that wood, a people tall and thin with white beards and sharp noses, like my grandfather. Before my grandfather ever replied to my many questions he would rub the tip of his nose with his forefinger; as for his beard, it was soft and luxuriant and as white as cotton-wool—never in my life have I seen anything of a purer whiteness or greater beauty. My grandfather must also have been extremely tall, for I never saw anyone in the whole area address him without having to look up at him, nor did I see him enter a house without having to bend so low that I was put in mind of the way the river wound round behind the wood of acacia trees. I loved him and would imagine myself, when I grew to be a man, tall and slender like him, walking along with great strides.

I believe I was his favourite grandchild: no wonder, for my cousins were a stupid bunch and I—so they say—was an intelligent child. I used to know when my grandfather wanted me to laugh, when to be silent; also I would remember the times for his prayers and would bring him his prayer-rug and fill the ewer for his ablutions without his having to ask me. When he had nothing else to do he enjoyed listening to me reciting to him from the Koran in a lilting voice, and I could tell from his face that he was moved.

One day I asked him about our neighbour Masood. I said to my grandfather: 'I fancy you don't like our neighbour Masood?'

To which he answered, having rubbed the tip of his nose: 'He's an indolent man and I don't like such people.'

I said to him: 'What's an indolent man?'

My grandfather lowered his head for a moment, then looking across at the wide expanse of field, he said: 'Do you see it stretching out from the edge of the desert up to the Nile bank? A hundred feddans. Do you see all those date palms? And those trees—sant, acacia, and sayal? All this fell into Masood's lap, was inherited by him from his father.'

Taking advantage of the silence that had descended upon my grandfather, I turned my gaze from him to the vast area defined by his words. 'I don't care,' I told myself, 'who owns those date palms, those trees or this black, cracked earth—all I know is that it's the arena for my dreams and my playground.'

My grandfather then continued: 'Yes, my boy, forty years ago all this belonged to Masood—two-thirds of it is now mine.'

This was news to me for I had imagined that the land had belonged to my grandfather ever since God's Creation.

'I didn't own a single feddan when I first set foot in this village. Masood was then the owner of all these riches. The position has changed now, though, and I think that before Allah calls to Him I shall have bought the remaining third as well.'

I do not know why it was I felt fear at my grandfather's words—and pity for our neighbour Masood. How I wished my grandfather wouldn't do what he'd said! I remembered Masood's singing, his beautiful voice and powerful laugh that resembled the gurgling of water. My grandfather never used to laugh.

I asked my grandfather why Masood had sold his land.

'Women,' and from the way my grandfather pronounced the word I felt that 'women' was something terrible. 'Masood, my boy, was a much-married man. Each time he married he sold me a feddan or two.' I made the quick calculation that Masood must have married some ninety women. Then I remembered his three wives, his shabby appearance, his lame donkey and its dilapidated saddle, his djellaba with the torn sleeves. I had all but rid my mind of the thoughts that jostled in it when I saw the man approaching us, and my grandfather and I exchanged glances.

'We'll be harvesting the dates today,' said Masood. 'Don't you want to be there?'

I felt, though, that he did not really want my grandfather to attend. My grandfather, however, jumped to his feet and I saw that his eyes sparkled momentarily with an intense brightness. He pulled me by the hand and we went off to the harvesting of Masood's dates.

Someone brought my grandfather a stool covered with an ox-hide, while I remained standing. There was a vast number of people there, but though I knew them all, I found myself for some reason, watching Masood: aloof from the great gathering of people he stood as though it were no concern of his, despite the fact that the date palms to be harvested were his own. Sometimes his attention would be caught by the sound of a huge clump of dates crashing down from on high. Once he shouted up at the boy perched on the very summit of the date palm who had begun hacking at a clump with his long, sharp sickle: 'Be careful you don't cut the heart of the palm.'

No one paid any attention to what he said and the boy seated at the very summit of the date palm continued, quickly

and energetically, to work away at the branch with his sickle
till the clump of dates began to drop like something descend-
ing from the heavens.

I, however, had begun to think about Masood's phrase 'the
heart of the palm'. I pictured the palm tree as something with
feeling, something possessed of a heart that throbbed. I remembered Masood's remark to me when he had once seen me
playing about with the branch of a young palm tree: 'Palm
trees, my boy, like humans, experience joy and suffering.'
And I had felt an inward and unreasoned embarrassment.

When I again looked at the expanse of ground stretching
before me I saw my young companions swarming like ants
around the trunks of the palm trees, gathering up dates and
eating most of them. The dates were collected into high
mounds. I saw people coming along and weighing them into
measuring bins and pouring them into sacks, of which I
counted thirty. The crowd of people broke up, except for
Hussein the merchant, Mousa the owner of the field next to
ours on the east, and two men I'd never seen before.

I heard a low whistling sound and saw that my grandfather
had fallen asleep. Then I noticed that Masood had not changed
his stance, except that he had placed a stalk in his mouth and
was munching at it like someone surfeited with food who
doesn't know what to do with the mouthful he still has.

Suddenly my grandfather woke up, jumped to his feet and
walked towards the sacks of dates. He was followed by Hussein the merchant, Mousa the owner of the field next to ours,
and the two strangers. I glanced at Masood and saw that he
was making his way towards us with extreme slowness, like a
man who wants to retreat but whose feet insist on going
forward. They formed a circle round the sacks of dates and
began examining them, some taking a date or two to eat. My
grandfather gave me a fistful, which I began munching. I saw
Masood filling the palms of both hands with dates and bringing them up close to his nose, then returning them.

Then I saw them dividing up the sacks between them.
Hussein the merchant took ten; each of the strangers took five.
Mousa the owner of the field next to ours on the eastern side
took five, and my grandfather took five. Understanding

nothing, I looked at Masood and saw that his eyes were darting about to left and right like two mice that have lost their way home.

'You're still fifty pounds in debt to me,' said my grandfather to Masood. 'We'll talk about it later.'

Hussein called his assistants and they brought along donkeys, the two strangers produced camels, and the sacks of dates were loaded on to them. One of the donkeys let out a braying which set the camels frothing at the mouth and complaining noisily. I felt myself drawing close to Masood, felt my hand stretch out towards him as though I wanted to touch the hem of his garment. I heard him make a noise in his throat like the rasping of a lamb being slaughtered. For some unknown reason, I experienced a sharp sensation of pain in my chest.

I ran off into the distance. Hearing my grandfather call after me, I hesitated a little, then continued on my way. I felt at that moment that I hated him. Quickening my pace, it was as though I carried within me a secret I wanted to rid myself of. I reached the river bank near the bend it made behind the wood of acacia trees. Then, without knowing why, I put my finger into my throat and spewed up the dates I'd eaten.

A Conversation from the Third Floor

Mohamed El-Bisatie
translated by Denys Johnson-Davies

She came to the place for the second time. The policeman
stared down at her from his horse.

The time was afternoon. The yellow-coloured wall stretched
right along the road. Inside the wall was a large rectangular
three-storey building; its small identical windows looked more
like dark apertures. The woman stood a few paces away from
the horse. The policeman looked behind him at the windows,
then at the woman. He placed both hands on the pommel of
the saddle and closed his eyes. After a while the horse moved.
It was standing halfway down the street. Then, a moment
later, it made a half-turn and once again stood itself at the top
of the street.

The woman came two steps forward. The horse bent one of
its forelegs, then gently lowered it.

'Sergeant, please, just let me say two words to him.'

His eyes remained closed, his hands motionless on the
pommel.

Above the wall stretched a fencing of barbed wire at the end
of which was a wooden tower. Inside there stood an armed
soldier.

The woman took another step forward.

'You see, he's been transferred. . .'

The sun had passed beyond the central point in the sky.
Despite this the weather was still hot. A narrow patch of shade
lay at the bottom of the wall.

The woman transferred the child to her shoulder.

When she again looked at the policeman's face, she noticed
thin lines of sweat on his forehead.

Quietly she moved away from in front of the horse and walked beside the wall. About halfway along it she sat down on a heap of stones opposite the building.

The prisoners' washing, hung by the arms and legs, could be seen outside the bars of the windows. Mostly it was completely motionless, even with the breeze that blew from time to time.

The woman whispered to herself: 'They must be wet.'

She placed the child in her lap. For a moment her eyes fastened on a djellaba that gently swayed to the movement of the wind. She stretched out her leg and gazed at her toes and the dried mud that clung to them. She rubbed her feet together, then gazed at them once again.

Putting back her head, she looked up at the windows of the third floor with half-closed eyes.

The soldier in the tower took a step forward. He rested his head against the edge of the wooden wall.

He looked at the sky, at the roofs of the houses, at the street, then at the head of the white horse.

Suddenly a shout broke the silence. The woman quickly drew back her leg. She caught sight of a bare arm waving from between the bars of a window on the third floor.

'Aziza! Aziza! It's Ashour.'

She moved a step nearer to the wall and stared in silence at the window.

'It's Ashour, Aziza. Ashour.'

She saw his other arm stretching out through the window. She searched with her eyes for something between the two arms and succeeded in making out a face pressed between the two bars. Other faces could be seen above and alongside him.

'Aziza, I've been transferred. Did you get my letter? In four days I'll be transferred. Did you prune the two date palms? Where are Hamid and Saniyya? Why didn't you bring them with you? I'm being transferred. Where's Hamid?'

He turned round suddenly, shouting:

'Stop it, you bastards!'

She heard him shouting and saw the faces disappear from the window. After a while his face was again looking out through the bars, then the other faces looked out above his.

'Aziza!'

She looked at the policeman on the horse, then at the soldier in the tower.

'Who are you holding? Shakir? Aziza!' She shook her head twice.

'Lift him up. Lift him up high.'

She took the child between her hands and lifted him above her head.

She noticed his arms suddenly being withdrawn inside and his hands gripping the iron bars of the window. Then his face disappeared from view. For a while she searched for him among the faces that looked down. She lowered her arms a little and heard shouts of laughter from the window. She spotted his arm once again stretching outwards, then his face appeared clearly in the middle.

'Up, Aziza. Up. Face him towards the sun so I can see him.'

She lowered her arms for a moment, then raised him up again, turning his face towards the sun. The child closed his eyes and burst out crying.

'He's crying.'

He turned round, laughing.

'The boy's crying! The little so-and-so! Aziza, woman, keep him crying!'

He cupped his hand round his mouth and shouted: 'Let him cry!'

Again he laughed. A few shouts went up around him. She heard their words and shoutings. Then she saw his large nose poking out through the bars.

'Woman! Don't be silly, that's enough! Cover the boy—he'll get sunstroke!'

She hugged the child to her chest and saw the soldier withdrawing inside the tower.

'Did you prune the two date palms?'

She shook her head.

'Why not? Why don't you talk? I'm being transferred. Pass by Abu Ismail and tell him I send him my best wishes—he'll do it as a favour and prune the trees, then you can bring along a few dates. Did you bring the cigarettes?'

She made a sign with her hand.

'Talk. What are you saying?'

'You've got 'em.'

'Louder, woman.'

'You've got 'em, I sent them to you.'

'When?'

'Just now.'

'Just now? Here, hang on—don't move.'

He disappeared suddenly. Two faces remained at the window. One of them stretched out his arm; he made an obscene movement in the air with his hand. She lowered her eyes, then went back to the pile of stones.

'Aziza!'

Though she did not recognise the voice, she looked up at the window. She saw the man was smiling, his arm still moving about. The second man was kneeling, having raised his djellaba above his thighs. She heard him call out:

'Aziza, look!'

She smiled. The policeman was still sitting on his horse as though asleep. From the side window of the tower she had a partial view of the soldier's head. He had taken off his helmet.

She heard several voices calling her. She listened attentively, concentrating her gaze on the soldier's head as he moved within the opening of the window. The calls were repeated, interspersed with abuse. The soldier put on his helmet, but remained inside the tower.

Suddenly the voices were silent and some moments later there came to her the breathless voice of her husband:

'Aziza? I said five—didn't I tell you five packets?' She stared up towards him in silence.

'Woman, what's the use of three packets?' She gestured to him with her hand.

'What are you saying?'

'Five—I sent five.'

'Five?' he shouted fiercely. 'The bastards!'

He disappeared suddenly, then leant out again shouting: 'Wait! Don't go!'

She turned her face towards the window of the tower. He was away for a while, then he returned.

'It's all right, Aziza. Never mind. Five—yes, there were five. Never mind, a couple got taken, it doesn't matter. Listen— what was I going to say?' Silence. She saw him staring out in silence from the window. She shook out her black djellaba and walked forward towards the wall. He smiled.

'Aziza, I was thinking of saying something to you.'

Again there was silence. She turned away her head so that part of her face was against the sun. She shifted her head-veil slightly from her head.

'They took a couple of packets. Never mind, Aziza. Never mind.'

He laughed. His voice had become calm. The other faces disappeared from above him, only a single face remaining alongside his.

'Did you build the wall?'

'Not yet.'

'Why not?'

'When Uncle Ahmed lights the furnace, I'll get some bricks from him.'

'All right. Be careful on the tram. Look after the boy.'

She remained standing.

'Anything you want?'

'No.'

She gazed at his face, his large nose, his bare arms. She smiled. The face next to his smiled back.

Suddenly he shouted. 'Did you get the letter? I'm being transferred.'

'Where to?'

'I don't know.'

'When?'

'You see, they're pulling down the prison.'

'Where will you go?'

'God knows—anywhere. No one knows.'

'When?'

'In two or three days. Don't come here again. I'll let you know when I'm transferred. Has the boy gone to sleep?'

'No, he's awake.'

He stared back for a while in silence.

'Aziza!'

Again there was silence. The face alongside his smiled, then slowly slid back inside and disappeared. Her husband remained silent, his arms around the bars.

Suddenly he glanced behind him and quickly drew in his

arms. He signalled to her to move away, then disappeared from the window.

She stepped back, though she remained standing looking up at the window.

After a while she seated herself on the stones and stretched out her leg. Taking out her breasts, she suckled her child.

The shadow advanced halfway across the street. She saw that its fringe was touching her foot. She drew her foot back a little. The place was quiet and the washing that had been hung out gently swayed in the breeze.

When she looked at her foot again, she saw that the shadow clothed the tips of her toes. She stood up.

The soldier was still inside the tower; the toe of his boot could be seen at the edge of the wooden platform. Before reaching where the horse stood she glanced behind her, but the window was empty.

She looked quietly at the policeman: his eyes were closed, his hands on the pommel of the saddle. The horse stood motionless.

She walked down the narrow passageway towards the main street.

SOUTHERN AFRICA

Papa, Snake & I

B.L. Honwana
translated by Dorothy Guedes

As soon as Papa left the table to read the newspaper in the sitting-room, I got up as well. I knew that Mama and the others would take a little longer, but I didn't feel like staying with them at all.

When I stood up, Mama looked at me and said, 'Come here, let me look at your eyes'.

I went towards her slowly, because when Mama calls us we never know whether she's cross or not. After she had lifted my lids with the index finger of her left hand to make a thorough examination, she looked down at her plate and I stood waiting for her to send me away or to say something. She finished chewing, swallowed, and picked up the bone in her fingers to peep through the cavity, shutting one eye. Then she turned to me suddenly with a bewildered look on her face.

'Your eyes are bloodshot, you're weak and you've lost your appetite.'

The way she spoke made me feel obliged to say that none of this was my fault or else that I didn't do it on purpose. All the others looked on very curiously to see what was going to happen.

Mama peered down the middle of the bone again. Then she began to suck it, shutting her eyes, and only stopped for a moment to say, 'Tomorrow you're going to take a laxative.'

As soon as the others heard this, they began eating again very quickly and noisily. Mama didn't seem to have anything else to say, so I went out into the yard.

It was hot everywhere, and I could see no-one on the road. Over the back wall three oxen gazed at me. They must have come back from the water trough at the Administration and stayed to rest in the shade. Far away, over the oxen's horns, the grey tufts of the dusty thorn trees trembled like flames. Everything vibrated in the distance, and heat waves could even be seen rising from the stones in the road. Sartina was sitting on a straw mat in the shade of the house, eating her lunch. Chewing slowly, she looked around, and from time to time, with a careless gesture, she shooed away the fowls who came close to her hoping for crumbs. Even so, every now and then one of the bolder ones would jump on to the edge of the plate and run off with a lump of mealie meal in its beak, only to be pursued by the others. In their wild dispute, the lump would become so broken up that in the end even the smallest chicken would get its bit to peck.

When she saw me coming near, Sartina pulled her capulana down over her legs, and even then kept her hand spread out in front of her knees, firmly convinced that I wanted to peep at something. When I looked away she still didn't move her hand.

Toto came walking along slowly with his tongue hanging out, and went to the place where Sartina was sitting. He sniffed the plate from afar and turned away, taking himself off to the shade of the wall where he looked for a soft place to lie down. When he found one, he curled round with his nose almost on his tail, and only lay still when his stomach touched the ground. He gave a long yawn, and dropped his head between his paws. He wriggled a little, making sure that he was in the most comfortable position, then covered his ears with his paws.

When she had finished eating, Sartina looked at me insistently before removing her hand which covered the space between her knees, and only when she was sure I was not looking did she spring to her feet with a jump. The plate was so clean that it shone, but after darting a last suspicious glance at me, she took it to the trough. She moved languidly, swaying from the waist as her hips rose and fell under her capulana. She bent over the trough, but the back of her legs was exposed in this position, so she went to the other side for me not to see.

Mama appeared at the kitchen door, still holding the bone in her hand, and before calling Sartina to clear the table, she looked around to see if everything was in order. 'Don't forget to give Toto his food,' she said in Ronga.

Sartina went inside, drying her hands on her capulana, and afterwards came out with a huge pile of plates. When she came out the second time she brought the table-cloth and shook it on the stairs. While the fowls were skirmishing for the crumbs, pecking and squawking at each other, she folded it in two, four, and eight, and then went back inside. When she came out again she brought the aluminium plate with Toto's food, and put it on the cement cover of the water meter. Toto didn't have to be called to eat and even before the plate was put down, he threw himself on his food. He burrowed into the pile of rice with his nose, searching for the bits of meat which he gulped up greedily as he found them. When no meat was left, he pushed the bones aside and ate some rice. The fowls were all around him, but they didn't dare to come nearer because they knew very well what Toto was like when he was eating.

When he had swallowed the rice, Toto pretended he didn't want any more and went to sit in the shade of the sugar cane, waiting to see what the fowls would do. They came nervously towards his food, and risked a peck or two, very apprehensively. Toto watched this without making a single movement. Encouraged by the passivity of the dog, the fowls converged on the rice with great enthusiasm, creating an awful uproar. It was then that Toto threw himself on the heap, pawing wildly in all directions and growling like an angry lion. When the fowls disappeared, fleeing to all corners of the yard, Toto went back to the shade of the sugar cane, waiting for them to gather together again.

Before going to work Papa went to look at the chicken run with Mama. They both appeared at the kitchen door, Mama already wearing her apron and Papa with a toothpick in his mouth and his newspaper under his arm. When they passed me Papa was saying, 'It's impossible, it's impossible, things can't go on like this.'

I went after them, and when we entered the chicken run Mama turned to me as if she wanted to say something, but then she changed her mind and went towards the wire netting. There were all sorts of things piled up behind the chicken run: pipes left over from the building of the windmill on the farm, blocks which were bought when Papa was still thinking of making out-houses of cement, boxes, pieces of wood, and who knows what else. The fowls sometimes crept in amongst these things and laid their eggs where Mama couldn't reach them. On one side of the run lay a dead fowl, and Mama pointed to it and said, 'Now there's this one, and I don't know how many others have just died from one day to the next. The chickens simply disappear, and the eggs too. I had this one left here for you to see. I'm tired of talking to you about this, and you still don't take any notice.'

'All right, all right, but what do you want me to do about it?'

'Listen, the fowls die suddenly, and the chickens disappear. No one goes into the chicken run at night, and we've never heard any strange noise. You must find out what's killing the fowls and chickens.'

'What do you think it is?'

'The fowls are bitten and the chickens are eaten. It can only be the one thing you think it is—if there are any thoughts in your head.'

'All right, tomorrow I'll get the snake killed. It's Sunday, and it will be easy to get people to do it. Tomorrow.'

Papa was already going out of the chicken run when Mama said, now in Portuguese, 'But tomorrow without fail, because I don't want any of my children bitten by a snake.'

Papa had already disappeared behind the corner of the house on his way to work when Mama turned to me and said, 'Haven't you ever been taught that when your father and mother are talking you shouldn't stay and listen! My children aren't usually so bad mannered. Who do you take after?'

She turned on Sartina, who was leaning against the wire netting and listening. 'What do you want? Did anyone call you? I'm talking to my son and it's none of your business.'

Sartina couldn't have grasped all that because she didn't understand Portuguese very well, but she drew away from the netting, looking very embarrassed, and went to the trough again. Mama went on talking to me, 'If you think you'll fool me and take the gun to go hunting you're making a big mistake. Heaven help you if you try to do a thing like that! I'll tan your backside for you! And if you think you'll stay here in the chicken run you're also mistaken. I don't feel like putting up with any of your nonsense, d'you hear?'

B.L. Honwana

Mama must have been very cross, because for the whole day
I hadn't heard her laugh as she usually did. After talking to me
she went out of the chicken run and I followed her. When she
passed Sartina, she asked her in Ronga, 'Is it very hot under
your capulana? Who told you to come here and show your legs
to everybody?'

Sartina said nothing, walked round the trough and went on
washing the plates, bending over the other side.

Mama went away and I went to sit where I had been before.
When Sartina saw me she turned on me resentfully, threw me
a furious glance, and went round the trough again. She began
to sing a monotonous song, one of those songs of hers that she
sometimes spent the whole afternoon singing over and over
again when she was angry.

Toto was bored with playing with the fowls, and had already
finished eating his rice. He was sleeping again with his paws
over his ears. Now and then he rolled himself in the dust and
lay on his back with his legs folded in the air.

It was stiflingly hot, and I didn't know whether I'd go
hunting as I usually did every Saturday, or if I'd go to the
chicken run to see the snake.

Madunana came into the yard with a pile of firewood on his
back, and went to put it away in the corner where Sartina was
washing the plates. When she saw him, she stopped singing
and tried to manage an awkward smile.

After looking all around, Madunana pinched Sartina's bottom, and she gave an embarrassed giggle and responded with
a sonorous slap on his arm. The two of them laughed happily
together without looking at each other.

Just then, Nandito, Joãozinho, Nelita and Gita ran out after
a ball, and started kicking it around the yard with great
enjoyment.

Mama came to the kitchen door, dressed up to go out. As
soon as she appeared, Madunana bent down quickly to the
ground, pretending to look for something, and Sartina bent
over the trough.

'Sartina, see if you manage not to break any plates before
you finish. Hurry up. You Madunana, leave Sartina alone and
mind your own business. I don't want any of that nonsense

here. If you carry on like this I'll tell the boss.'

'You, Ginho,' (now she spoke in Portuguese) 'Look after the
house and remember you're not a child any more. Don't hit
anybody and don't let the children go out of the yard. Tina and
Lolota are inside clearing up—don't let them get up to mis-
chief.'

'Sartina,' (in Ronga) 'When you've finished with that put the
kettle on for the children's tea and tell Madunana to go and
buy bread. Don't let the children finish the whole packet of
butter.'

'Ginho,' (now in Portuguese) 'Look after everything—I'm
coming back just now. I'm going along to Aunty Lucia's for a
little chat.'

Mama straightened her dress and looked around to see if
everything was in order, then went away.

Senhor Castro's dog, Wolf, was watching Toto from the
street. As soon as he saw Wolf, Toto ran towards him and they
started to bark at each other.

All the dogs of the village were frightened of Toto, and even
the biggest of them ran away when he showed his temper.
Toto was small, but he had long white hair which bristled up
like a cat's when he was angry, and this is what must have
terrified the other dogs.

Usually he kept away from them, preferring to entertain
himself with the fowls—even bitches he only tolerated at
certain times. For me he was a dog with a 'pedigree', or at least
'pedigree' could only mean the qualities he possessed. He had
an air of authority, and the only person he feared was Mama,
although she had never hit him. Just to take him off a chair we
had to call her because he snarled and showed his teeth even at
Papa.

The two dogs were face to face, and Wolf had already started
to retreat, full of fear. At this moment Dr Reis's dog, Kiss,
passed by, and Toto started to bark at him too. Kiss fled at
once, and Wolf pursued him, snapping at his hind-quarters,
only leaving him when he was whining with pain. When Wolf
came back to Toto they immediately made friends and began
playing together.

Nandito came and sat down next to me, and told me, without

my asking, that he was tired of playing ball.

'So why have you come here?'

'Don't you want me to?'

'I didn't say that.'

'Then I'll stay.'

'Stay if you like.'

I got up and he followed me. 'Where are you going? Are you going hunting?'

'No.'

'Well, then?'

'Stop pestering me. I don't like talking to kids.'

'You're also a kid. Mama still hits you.'

'Say that again and I'll bash your face in.'

'All right, I won't say it again.'

I went into the chicken run, and he came after me. The pipes were hot, and I had to move them with a cloth. The dust that rose was dense and suffocating.

'What are you looking for? Shall I help you?'

I began to move the blocks one by one and Nandito did the same. 'Get away!'

He went to the other end of the run and began to cry.

When I had removed the last block of the pile I saw the snake. It was a mamba, very dark in colour. When it realised it had been discovered it wound itself up more tightly and lifted its triangular head. Its eyes shone vigilantly and its black forked tongue quivered menacingly.

I drew back against the fence, then sat down on the ground. 'Don't cry, Nandito.'

'You're nasty. You don't want to play with me.'

'Don't cry any more. I'll play with you just now. Don't cry.'

We both sat quietly. The little head of the snake came slowly to rest on the topmost coil, and the rest of its body stopped trembling. But it continued to watch me attentively.

'Nandito, say something, talk to me.'

'What do you want me to say?'

'Anything you like.'

'I don't feel like saying anything.'

Nandito was still rubbing his eyes and feeling resentful towards me.

'Have you ever seen a snake? Do you like snakes? Are you

scared of them? Answer me!'

'Where are the snakes?' Nandito jumped up in terror, and looked around.

'In the bush. Sit down and talk.'

'Aren't there any snakes here?'

'No. Talk. Talk to me about snakes.'

Nandito sat down very close to me.

'I'm very frightened of snakes. Mama says it's dangerous to go out in the bush because of them. When we're walking in the grass we can step on one by mistake and get bitten. When a snake bites us we die. Sartina says that if a snake bites us and we don't want to die we must kill it, burn it till it's dry, then eat it. She says she's already eaten a snake, so she won't die even if she gets bitten.'

'Have you ever seen a snake?'

'Yes, in Chico's house. The servant killed it in the chicken run.'

'What was it like?'

'It was big and red, and it had a mouth like a frog.'

'Would you like to see a snake now?'

Nandito got up and leaned against me fearfully. 'Is there a snake in the chicken run? I'm scared—let's get out.'

'If you want to get out, go away. I didn't call you to come in here.'

'I'm frightened to go alone.'

'Then sit here until I feel like going out.'

The two of us stayed very quietly for a while.

Toto and Wolf were playing outside the fence. They were running from one post to another, going all the way round and starting again. At every post they raised a leg and urinated.

Then they came inside the chicken run and lay on their stomachs to rest. Wolf saw the snake immediately and began to bark. Toto barked as well, although he had his back turned towards it.

'Brother, are there always snakes in every chicken run?'

'No.'

'Is there one in here?'

'Yes.'

'Well then, why don't we go out. I'm scared!'

'Go out if you want to—go on!'

Wolf advanced towards the snake, barking more and more frenziedly. Toto turned his head, but still did not realise what was wrong.

Wolf's legs were trembling and he pawed the ground in anguish. Now and again he looked at me uncomprehendingly, unable to understand why I did not react to his hysterical alarm. His almost human eyes were filled with panic.

'Why is he barking like that?'

'Because he's seen the snake.'

The mamba was curled up in the hollow between some blocks, and it unwound its body to give itself the most solid support possible. Its head and the raised neck remained poised in the air, unaffected by the movement of the rest of its body. Its eyes shone like fires.

Wolf's appeals were now horribly piercing, and his hair was standing up around his neck.

Leaning against the fence, Tina and Lolota and Madunana looked on curiously.

'Why don't you kill the snake?' Nandito's voice was very tearful and he was clutching me around the neck.

'Because I don't feel like it.'

The distance between the snake and the dog was about five feet. However, the snake had inserted its tail in the angle formed between a block and the ground, and had raised its coils one by one, preparing for the strike. The triangular head drew back imperceptibly, and the base of the lifted neck came forward. Seeming to be aware of the promixity of his end, the dog began to bark even more frantically, without, however, trying to get away from the snake. From a little way behind, Toto, now on his feet as well, joined in the barking.

For a fraction of a second the neck of the snake curved while the head leaned back. Then, as if the tension of its pliant body had snapped a cord that fastened its head to the ground, it shot forward in a lightning movement impossible to follow. Although the dog had raised himself on his hind legs like a goat, the snake struck him full on the chest. Free of support, the tail of the snake whipped through the air, reverberating with the movement of the last coil.

Wolf fell on his back with a suppressed whine, pawing convulsively. The mamba abandoned him immediately, and with a spring disappeared between the pipes.

'A nhoka!'[1] screamed Sartina.

Nandito threw me aside and ran out of the chicken run with a yell, collapsing into the arms of Madunana. As soon as he felt free of the snake, Wolf vanished in half a dozen leaps in the direction of Senhor Castro's house.

The children all started to cry without having understood what had happened. Sartina took Nandito to the house, carrying him in her arms. Only when the children disappeared behind Sartina did I call Madunana to help me kill the snake.

Madunana waited with a cloth held up high while I moved the pipes with the aid of a broomstick. As soon as the snake appeared Mandunana threw the cloth over it, and I set to beating the heap with my stick.

When Papa came back from work Nandito had come round from the shock, and was weeping copiously. Mama, who had not yet been to see the snake, went with Papa to the chicken run. When I went there as well, I saw Papa turn the snake over on to its back with a stick.

'I don't like to think of what a snake like this could have done to one of my children.' Papa smiled. 'Or to anyone else. It was better this way. What hurts me is to think that these six feet of snake were attained at the expense of my chickens. . .'

At this point Senhor Castro's car drew up in front of our house. Papa walked up to him, and Mama went to talk to Sartina. I followed after Papa.

'Good afternoon, Senhor Castro. . .'

'Listen, Tchembene, I've just found out that my pointer is dead, and his chest's all swollen. My natives tell me that he came howling from your house before he died. I don't want any back-chat, and I'm just telling you—either you pay compensation or I'll make a complaint at the Administration. He was the best pointer I ever had.'

'I've just come back from work—I don't know anything. . .'

'I don't care a damn about that. Don't argue. Are you going to pay or aren't you?'

'But Senhor Castro. . .'

'Senhor Castro nothing. It's 700 paus.[2] And it's better if the matter rests here.'

'As you like, Senhor Castro, but I don't have the money now. . .'

'We'll see about that later. I'll wait until the end of the month, and if you don't pay then there'll be a row.'

'Senhor Castro, we've known each other such a long time, and there's never. . .'

'Don't try that with me. I know what you all need—a bloody good hiding is the only thing. . .'

Senhor Castro climbed into his car and pulled away. Papa stayed watching while the car drove off. 'Son of a bitch. . .'

I went up to him and tugged at the sleeve of his coat.

'Papa, why didn't you say that to his face?'

He didn't answer.

We had hardly finished supper when Papa said, 'Mother, tell Sartina to clear the table quickly. My children, let us pray. To-day we are not going to read the Bible. We will simply pray.'

Papa talked in Ronga, and for this reason I regretted having asked him that question a while ago.

When Sartina finished clearing away the plates and folded the cloth, Papa began, *'Tatana, ha ku dumba hosi ya tilo misaba. . .'*[3]

When he finished, his eyes were red.

'Amen!'

'Amen!'

Mama got up, and asked, as if it meant nothing, 'But what did Senhor Castro want, after all?'

'It's nothing important.'

'All right, tell me about it in our room. I'll go and set out the children's things. You, Ginho, wake up early tomorrow and take a laxative . . .'

When they had all gone away, I asked Papa, 'Papa, why do you always pray when you are very angry?'

'Because He is the best counsellor.'

'And what counsel does He give you?'

'He gives me no counsel. He gives me strength to continue.'

'Papa, do you believe a lot in Him?'

Papa looked at me as if he were seeing me for the first time, and then exploded. 'My son, one must have a hope. When one

comes to the end of a day, and one knows that tomorrow will
be another day just like it, and that things will always be the
same, we have got to find the strength to keep on smiling, and
keep on saying, "This is not important!" We ourselves have to
allot our own reward for the heroism of every day. We have to
establish a date for this reward, even if it's the day of our death!
Even today you saw Senhor Castro humiliate me: this formed
only part of today's portion, because there were many things
that happened that you didn't see. No, my son, there must be
a hope! It must exist! Even if all this only denies Him, He must
exist!'

Papa stopped suddenly, and forced himself to smile. Then
he added, 'Even a poor man has to have something. Even if it is
only a hope! Even if it's a false hope!'

'Papa, I could have prevented the snake from biting Senhor
Castro's dog. . .'

Papa looked at me with his eyes full of tenderness, and said
under his breath, 'It doesn't matter. It's a good thing that he
got bitten.'

Mama appeared at the door. 'Are you going to let the child
go to sleep or not?'

I looked at Papa, and we remembered Senhor Castro and
both of us burst out laughing. Mama didn't understand.

'Are you two going crazy?!'

'Yes, and it's about time we went crazy,' said Papa with a
smile.

Papa was already on the way to his room, but I must have
talked too loudly. Anyway, it was better that he heard, 'Papa, I
sometimes . . . I don't really know . . . but for some time . . . I
have been thinking that I didn't love you all. I'm sorry. . .'

Mama didn't understand what we had been saying, so she
became angry. 'Stop all this, or else . . .'

'Do you know, my son,' Papa spoke ponderously, and
gesticulated a lot before every word. 'The most difficult thing
to bear is that feeling of complete emptiness . . . and one
suffers very much . . . very, very, very much. One grows with
so much bottled up inside, but afterwards it is difficult to
scream, you know.'

'Papa, and when Senhor Castro comes? . . .'

Mama was going to object, but Papa clutched her shoulder

firmly. 'It's nothing, Mother, but, you know, our son believes that people don't mount wild horses, and that they only make use of the hungry, docile ones. Yet when a horse goes wild it gets shot down, and it's all finished. But tame horses die every day. Every day, d'you hear? Day after day, after day—as long as they can stand on their feet.'

Mama looked at him with her eyes popping out.

'Do you know, Mother, I'm afraid to believe that this is true, but I also can't bring myself to tell him that it's a lie . . . He sees, even to-day he saw . . . I only wish for the strength to make sure that my children know how to recognise other things . . .'

Papa and Mama were already in their room, so I couldn't hear any more, but even from there Mama yelled, 'Tomorrow you'll take a laxative, that'll show you. I'm not like your father who lets himself get taken in . . .'

My bed was flooded in yellow moonlight, and it was pleasant to feel my naked skin quiver with its cold caress. For some unknown reason the warm sensation of Sartina's body flowed through my senses. I managed to cling to her almost physical presence for a few minutes, and I wanted to fall asleep with her so as not to dream of dogs and snakes.

1. nhoka—a snake
2. 700 'paus'—slang for 700$ (about £8)
3. *Tatana, ha ku dumba hosi ya tilo misaba*—Father, we put our trust in Thee, Lord of Heaven and earth

The Bridegroom

Nadine Gordimer

He came into his road camp that afternoon for the last time. It
was neater than any house would ever be; the sand raked
smooth in the clearing, the water drums under the tarpaulin,
the flaps of his tent closed against the heat. Thirty yards away a
black woman knelt, pounding mealies, and two or three
children, grey with Kalahari dust, played with a skinny dog.
Their shrillness was no more than a bird's piping in the great
spaces in which the camp was lost.

Inside his tent, something of the chill of the night before
always remained, stale but cool, like the air of a church. There
was his iron bed, with its clean pillowcase and big kaross.
There was his table, his folding chair with the red canvas seat,
and the chest in which his clothes were put away. Standing on
the chest was the alarm clock that woke him at five every
morning and the photograph of a seventeen-year-old girl from
Francistown whom he was going to marry. They had been
there a long time, the girl and the alarm clock; in the morning
when he opened his eyes, in the afternoon when he came off
the job. But now this was the last time. He was leaving for
Francistown in the Roads Department ten-tonner, in the
morning; when he came back, the next week, he would be
married and he would have with him the girl, and the caravan
which the department provided for married men. He had his
eye on her as he sat down on the bed and took off his boots; the
smiling girl was like one of those faces cut out of a magazine.
He began to shed his working overalls, a rind of khaki stiff
with dust that held his shape as he discarded it, and he called,
easily and softly, 'Ou Piet, ek wag.' But the bony black man with
his eyebrows raised like a clown's, in effort, and his bare feet
shuffling under the weight, was already at the tent with a tin
bath in which hot water made a twanging tune as it slopped
from side to side.

When he had washed and put on a clean khaki shirt and a pair of worn grey trousers, and streaked back his hair with sweet-smelling pomade, he stepped out of his tent just as the lid of the horizon closed on the bloody eye of the sun. It was winter and the sun set shortly after five; the grey sand turned a fading pink, the low thorn scrub gave out spreading stains of lilac shadow that presently all ran together; then the surface of the desert showed pocked and pored, for a minute or two, like the surface of the moon through a telescope, while the sky remained light over the darkened earth and the clean crystal pebble of the evening star shone. The campfires—his own and the black men's, over there—changed from near-invisible flickers of liquid colour to brilliant focuses of leaping tongues of light; it was dark. Every evening he sat like this through the short ceremony of the closing of the day, slowly filling his pipe, slowly easing his back round to the fire, yawning off the stiffness of his labour. Suddenly he gave a smothered giggle, to himself, of excitement. Her existence became real to him; he saw the face of the photograph, posed against a caravan door. He got up and began to pace about the camp, alert to promise. He kicked a log farther into the fire, he called an order to Piet, he walked up towards the tent and then changed his mind and strolled away again. In their own encampment at the edge of his, the road gang had taken up the exchange of laughing, talking, yelling, and arguing that never failed them when their work was done. Black arms gestured under a thick foam of white soap, there was a gasp and splutter as a head broke the cold force of a bucketful of water, the gleaming bellies of iron cooking pots were carried here and there in a talkative preparation of food. He did not understand much of what they were saying—he knew just enough Tswana to give them his orders, with help from Piet and one or two others who understood his own tongue, Afrikaans—but the sound of their voices belonged to this time of evening. One of the babies who always cried was keeping up a thin, ignored wail; the naked children were playing the chasing game that made the dog bark. He came back and sat down again at the fire, to finish his pipe.

After a certain interval (it was exact, though it was not timed by a watch, but by long habit that had established the appropriate lapse of time between his bath, his pipe, and his food) he called out, in Afrikaans, 'Have you forgotten my dinner, man?'

From across the patch of distorted darkness where the light of the two fires did not meet, but flung wobbling shapes and opaque, overlapping radiances, came the hoarse, protesting laugh that was, better than the tribute to a new joke, the pleasure in constancy to an old one.

Then a few minutes later: 'Piet! I suppose you've burned everything, eh?'

'Baas?'

'Where's the food, man?'

In his own time the black man appeared with the folding table and an oil lamp. He went back and forth between the dark and light, bringing pots and dishes and food, and nagging with deep satisfaction, in a mixture of English and Afrikaans. 'You want koeksusters, so I make koeksusters. You ask me this morning. So I got to make the oil nice and hot, I got to get everything ready . . . It's a little bit slow. Yes, I know. But I can't get everything quick, quick. You hurry tonight, you don't want wait, then it's better you have koeksusters on Saturday, then I'm got time in the afternoon, I do it nice. . . Yes, I think next time it's better . . .'

Piet was a good cook. 'I've taught my boy how to make everything', the young man always told people, back in Francistown. 'He can even make koeksusters', he had told the girl's mother, in one of those silences of the woman's disapproval that it was so difficult to fill. He had had a hard time, trying to overcome the prejudice of the girl's parents against the sort of life he could offer her. He had managed to convince them that the life was not impossible, and they had given their consent to the marriage, but they still felt that the life was unsuitable, and his desire to please and reassure them had made him anxious to see it with their eyes and so forestall, by changes, their objections. The girl was a farm girl, and would not pine for town life, but, at the same time, he could not deny to her parents that living on a farm with her family around her, and neighbours only thirty or forty miles away, would be very different from living two hundred and twenty miles from a town or village, alone with him in a road camp 'surrounded by a gang of kaffirs all day', as her mother had said. He himself

simply did not think at all about what the girl would do while
he was out on the road; and as for the girl, until it was over,
nothing could exist for her but the wedding, with her two little
sisters in pink walking behind her, and her dress that she
didn't recognise herself in, being made at the dressmaker's,
and the cake that was ordered with a tiny china bride and
groom in evening dress, on the top.

He looked at the scored table, and the rim of the open jam
tin, and the salt cellar with a piece of brown paper tied neatly
over the broken top, and said to Piet, 'You must do everything
nice when the missus comes.'

'Baas?'

They looked at each other and it was not really necessary to
say anything.

'You must make the table properly and do everything clean.'

'Always I make everything clean. Why you say now I must
make clean . . .'

The young man bent his head over his food, dismissing him.

While he ate his mind went automatically over the changes
that would have to be made for the girl. He was not used to
visualizing situations, but to dealing with what existed. It was
like a lesson learned by rote; he knew the totality of what was
needed, but if he found himself confronted by one of the
component details, he foundered: he did not recognise it or
know how to deal with it. The boys must keep out of the way.
That was the main thing. Piet would have to come to the
caravan quite a lot, to cook and clean. The boys—especially the
boys who were responsible for the maintenance of the lorries
and road-making equipment—were always coming with questions, what to do about this and that. They'd mess things up,
otherwise. He spat out a piece of gristle he could not swallow;
his mind went to something else. The women over there—
they could do the washing for the girl. They were such a raw
bunch of kaffirs, would they ever be able to do anything right?
Twenty boys and above five of their women—you couldn't
hide them under a thorn bush. They just mustn't hang around,
that's all. They must just understand that they mustn't hang
around. He looked round keenly through the shadow-
puppets of the half-dark on the margin of his fire's light; the
voices, companionably quieter, now, intermittent over food,

the echoing *chut!* of wood being chopped, the thin film of a baby's wail through which all these sounded—they were on their own side. Yet he felt an odd, rankling suspicion.

His thoughts shuttled, as he ate, in a slow and painstaking way that he had never experienced before in his life—he was worrying. He sucked on a tooth; Piet, Piet, that kaffir talks such a hell of a lot. How's Piet going to stop talking, talking every time he comes near? If he talks to her . . . Man, it's sure he'll talk to her. He thought, in actual words, what he would say to Piet about this; the words were like those unsayable things that people write on walls for others to see in private moments, but that are never spoken in their mouths.

Piet brought coffee and koeksusters and the young man did not look at him.

But the koeksusters were delicious, crisp, sticky, and sweet, and as he felt the familiar substance and taste on his tongue, alternating with the hot bite of the coffee, he at once became occupied with the pure happiness of eating as a child is fully occupied with a bag of sweets. Koeksusters never failed to give him this innocent, total pleasure. When first he had taken the job of overseer to the road gang, he had had strange, restless hours at night and on Sundays. It seemed that he was hungry. He ate but never felt satisfied. He walked about all the time, like a hungry creature. One Sunday he actually set out to walk (the Roads Department was very strict about the use of the ten-tonner for private purposes) the fourteen miles across the sand to the cattle-dipping post where the government cattle officer and his wife, Afrikaners like himself and the only other white people between the road camp and Francistown, lived in their corrugated-iron house. By a coincidence, they had decided to drive over and see him, that day, and they had met him a little less than halfway, when he was already slowed and dazed by heat. But shortly after that Piet had taken over the cooking of his meals and the care of his person, and Piet had even learned to make koeksusters, according to instructions given to the young man by the cattle officer's wife. The koeksusters, a childhood treat that he could indulge in whenever he liked, seemed to mark his settling down; the solitary camp became a personal way of life, with its own special arrangements and indulgences.

'*Ou Piet! Kêrel!* What did you do to the koeksusters, hey?' he called out joyously.

A shout came that meant 'Right away'. The black man appeared, drying his hands on a rag, with the diffident, kidding manner of someone who knows he has excelled himself.

'Whatsa matter with the koeksusters, man?'

Piet shrugged. 'You must tell me. I don't know what's matter.'

'Here, bring me some more, man.' The young man shoved the empty plate at him, with a grin. And as the other went off, laughing, the young man called. 'You must always make them like that, see?'

He liked to drink at celebrations, at weddings or Christmas, but he wasn't a man who drank his brandy every day. He would have two brandies on a Saturday afternoon, when the week's work was over, and for the rest of the time, the bottle that he brought from Francistown when he went to collect stores lay in the chest in his tent. But on this last night he got up from the fire on impulse and went over to the tent to fetch the bottle (one thing he didn't do, he didn't expect a kaffir to handle his drink for him; it was too much of a temptation to put in their way). He brought a glass with him, too, one of a set of six made of tinted imitation cut glass, and he poured himself a tot and stretched out his legs where he could feel the warmth of the fire through the soles of his boots. The nights were not cold, until the wind came up at two or three in the morning, but there was a clarifying chill to the air; now and then a figure came over from the black men's camp to put another log on the fire whose flames had dropped and become blue. The young man felt inside himself a similar low incandescence; he poured himself another brandy. The long yelping of the jackals prowled the sky without, like the wind about a house; there was no house, but the sounds beyond the light his fire trembl-ingly inflated into the dark—that jumble of meaningless voices, crying babies, coughs, and hawking—had built walls to enclose and a roof to shelter. He was exposed, turning naked to space on the sphere of the world as the speck that is a fly plastered on the window of an aeroplane, but he was not aware of it.

The lilt of various kinds of small music began and died in the dark; threads of notes, blown and plucked, that disappeared under the voices. Presently a huge man whose thick black body had strained apart every seam in his ragged pants and shirt loped silently into the light and dropped just within it, not too near the fire. His feet, intimately crossed, were cracked and weathered like driftwood. He held to his mouth a one-stringed instrument shaped like a lyre, made out of a half-moon of bent wood with a ribbon of dried palm leaf tied from tip to tip. His big lips rested gently on the strip and while he blew, his one hand, by controlling the vibration of the palm leaf, made of his breath a small, faint, perfect music. It was caught by the very limits of the capacity of the human ear; it was almost out of range. The first music men ever heard, when they began to stand upright among the rushes at the river, might have been like it. When it died away it was difficult to notice at what point it really had gone.

'Play that other one,' said the young man, in Tswana. Only the smoke from his pipe moved.

The pink-palmed hands settled down round the instrument. The thick, tender lips were wet once. The faint disolate voice spoke again, so lonely a music that it came to the player and listener as if they heard it inside themselves. This time the player took a short stick in his other hand and, while he blew, scratched it back and forth inside the curve of the lyre, where the notches cut there produced a dry, shaking, slithering sound, like the far-off movement of dancers' feet. There were two or three figures with more substance than the shadows, where the firelight merged with the darkness. They came and squatted. One of them had half a paraffin tin, with a wooden neck and other attachments of gut and wire. When the lyre-player paused, lowering his piece of stick and leaf slowly, in ebb, from his mouth, and wiping his lips on the back of his hand, the other began to play. It was a thrumming, repetitive, banjo tune. The young man's boot patted the sand in time to it and he took it up with hand-claps once or twice. A thin, yellowish man in an old hat pushed his way to the front past sarcastic remarks and twittings and sat on his haunches with a little clay bowl between his feet. Over its mouth there was a keyboard of metal tongues. After some exchange, he played it

and the others sang low and nasally, bringing a few more
strollers to the fire. The music came to an end, pleasantly, and
started up again, like a breath drawn. In one of the intervals
the young man said, 'Let's have a look at that contraption of
yours, isn't it a new one?' and the man to whom he signalled
did not understand what was being said to him but handed
over his paraffin-tin mandolin with pride and also with amuse-
ment at his own handiwork.

The young man turned it over, twanged it once, grinning
and shaking his head. Two bits of string and an old jam tin and
they'll make a whole band, man. He'd heard them playing
some crazy-looking things. The circle of faces watched him
with pleasure; they laughed and lazily remarked to each other;
it was a funny-looking thing, all right, but it worked. The
owner took it back and played it, clowning a little. The audience laughed and joked appreciatively; they were sitting close
in to the fire now, painted by it. 'Next week' the young man
raised his voice gaily—'next week when I come back, I bring
radio with me, plenty real music. All the big white bands play
over it . . .' Someone who had once worked in Johannesburg
said, 'Satchmo', and the others took it up, understanding that
this was the word for what the white man was going to bring
from town. Satchmo. Satch-mo. They tried it out, politely.
'Music, just like at a big white dance in town. Next week.' A
friendly, appreciative silence fell, with them all resting back in
the warmth of the fire and looking at him indulgently. A
strange thing happened to him. He felt hot, over first his neck,
then his ears and his face. It didn't matter, of course; by next
week they would have forgotten. They wouldn't expect it. He
shut down his mind on a picture of them, hanging round the
caravan to listen, and him coming out on the steps to tell
them . . .

He thought for a moment that he would give them the rest of
the bottle of brandy. Hell, no, man, it was mad. If they got the
taste for the stuff, they'd be pinching it all the time. He'd give
Piet some sugar and yeast and things from the stores, for them
to make beer tomorrow when he was gone. He put his hands
deep in his pockets and stretched out to the fire with his head
sunk on his chest. The lyre-player picked up his flimsy piece of
wood again, and slowly what the young man was feeling

inside himself seemed to find a voice; up into the night beyond the fire, it went, uncoiling from his breast and bringing ease. As if it had been made audible out of infinity and could be returned to infinity at any point, the lonely voice of the lyre went on and on. Nobody spoke, the barriers of tongues fell with silence. The whole dirty tide of worry and planning had gone out of the young man. The small, high moon, outshone by a spiky spread of cold stars, repeated the shape of the lyre. He sat for he was not aware how long, just as he had for so many other nights, with the stars at his head and the fire at his feet.

But at last the music stopped and time began again. There was tonight; there was tomorrow, when he was going to drive to Francistown. He stood up; the company fragmented. The lyre-player blew his nose into his fingers. Dusty feet took their accustomed weight. They went off to their tents and he went off to his. Faint plangencies followed them. The young man gave a loud, ugly, animal yawn, the sort of unashamed personal noise a man can make when he lives alone. He walked very slowly across the sand; it was dark but he knew the way more surely than with his eyes. 'Piet! Hey!' be bawled as he reached his tent. 'You get up early tomorrow, eh? And I don't want to hear the lorry won't start. You get it going and then you call me. D'you hear?'

He was lighting the oil lamp that Piet had left ready on the chest and as it came up softly it brought the whole interior of the tent with it: the chest, the bed, the clock, and the coy smiling face of the seventeen-year-old girl. He sat down on the bed, sliding his palms through the silky fur of the kaross. He drew a breath and held it for a moment, looking round purposefully. And then he picked up the photograph, folded the cardboard support back flat to the frame, and put it in the chest with all his other things, ready for the journey.

The Betrayal

Ahmed Essop

When Dr Kamal closed his surgery door one Friday night, he felt that a door had closed on his past.

He was a tall slender man, mud-complexioned, with a balding cranium that gave him a distinguished scholarly appearance. He was not only a physician and a well-known politician, but a connoisseur and collector of works of art displaying the agony of the proletariat in fields and factories. His entire collection was on display in his gallery-cum-study at home. He had received his medical and political education in India; his ability at the game of cricket had also been developed in that country. He was a religious man and every Friday he would dutifully attend the mosque in Newtown to genuflect in prayer.

For days he had been enmeshed in a dilemma, which had originated when a new political group in Fordsburg proclaimed its inaugural meeting by means of notices stuck on walls and lamp-posts. The emergence of the group, mainly consisting of youth, posed a threat to the Orient Front of which Dr Kamal was the president. A successful public meeting could be the first stage in its growth into a powerful rival political body, a body that could in time eliminate the Orient Front as a representative organisation. There was also a personal threat. Dr Kamal had achieved the presidency of the Orient Front after years of patient waiting and he was afraid that his position would lose some of its lustre with the appearance of another political body. He was also the political mentor of the Fordsburg youth and felt that his prestige and status would suffer a reduction if the new group drew deserters from the Youth League of which he was the founder. There was only one way to stop the threat: the new group had to be crushed at its inaugural meeting. But . . . how was he to reconcile this action with the fact that he had been a professed disciple of Gandhi during his political life?

He drove in his small German car to the offices of the Orient Front in Park Road. At ten o'clock he was to address a clandestine meeting of members of the Youth League. He reached the building, parked his car at the entrance, and walked slowly up a flight of stairs.

Salim Rashid, chairman of the Youth League, was waiting for him.

'We are ready, Doc.'

'How many?'

'Forty-two.'

'Have you explained to them what they have to do?'

'Yes. You have only to say a few words to them.'

It had been Salim Rashid's idea that he should address the Youth League, after the doctor had discreetly suggested that the new political group should be annihilated, in accordance with the 'ethics of political survival', before it hatched something dangerous. Had he rejected the idea, Dr Kamal would have given Salim Rashid the impression that he was afraid. The young man's argument had been that a few words from their mentor, on the eve of the clash, would be sufficient to convince the members of the rightness of their action. In order to keep the doctor's role a secret he would arrange a nocturnal meeting.

Salim Rashid opened a door. It led into a large room with many chairs and several tables. Some members of the Youth League were talking in groups, others were outside on the balcony. There were portraits, rather crudely garish, of Gandhi on the walls.

'Friends, attention. Dr Kamal is here to address you.'

They settled down on the chairs. The doctor began:

'One of the most important duties of the Youth League—in fact it is part of its unwritten constitution—is to safeguard the integrity and retain the hegemony of its parent body the Orient Front, and prevent rival political organisations from trespassing on our traditional ground. You have a great responsibility towards the Indian people of this country. You cannot permit them to be divided. The despots will destroy us if we let this happen. Let me remind you that it has always been a thesis of mine that there is no essential conflict of principles between Gandhi and the Western political philosophers, that a violent revolt and a passive revolt are aspects of the dynamics of man's search for freedom.'

He paused for a moment, coughed into his clenched hand, and continued:

'You should always remember that you are not only a vital part of the Orient Front, but also the vanguard that must protect it from harm. Remember always that you have been chosen by history to shape the future of this country.'

Dr Kamal had done. The youths clapped their hands, then raised their fists and shouted a few belligerent slogans.

He left the premises immediately.

On his way home he decided to pass Gandhi Hall where the meeting was to be held the next day. His motive for passing by was rooted in a strange sudden notion that the new group too had decided to hold a secret nocturnal meeting. Fear inflamed the turbulence within him and he stopped his car, half-expecting to see a knot of people coming up the street to attend the meeting. But the street was deserted and the hall doors locked. A gust of wind rushed by, carrying with it a swarm of rasping papers. The irony of his role struck him with force. He, the professed disciple of Gandhi, had unleashed a demon that would profane the hall commemorative of the master's name.

He went home and locked himself in his study. This room had been the scene, in the early days when he had joined the Orient Front, of weekly lectures to the youth of Fordsburg under the title 'A Study of the Dynamics of Political Action and Political Truth', which had gained such popularity that the numbers swelled and he had formed the Youth League. Its members had come to look upon him as their oracle on political matters. In his study he had expounded to them the political philosophy of the 'triumvirate', Marx, Lenin and Gandhi. He had spoken with veneration of Gandhi's passive resistance campaigns against the 'racist oligarchs' and had extolled him as a 'Titan in the history of humanity' as he had been the first to bring into the realm of politics the concepts of truth and non-violence. He had also proudly told the youth of his meetings with Gandhi while he was a medical student in India and his abandonment of radical and revolutionary ideas in politics.

When Dr Kamal took his seat in the hall he saw that it was packed with people. He felt his chest contract and he hurriedly lit a cigarette.

'Hullo, Doc,' said Rhada, the secretary of the Orient Front, sitting down beside him. 'Is our Youth League present?'

'This should be an interesting meeting,' he commented, pretending not to have heard the question.

'This should be their first and last meeting.'

Dr Kamal was jolted. So the secretary knew of the intentions of the Youth League? Salim Rashid had assured him that the plans were all secret and that he would not be implicated. Now someone had told the secretary—and perhaps many others— and though he seemed to approve of the planned disruption and violence there was no way of telling how he would react if things went wrong.

'There is Salim Rashid,' Rhada said, pointing towards the front.

'Yes,' Dr Kamal answered feebly.

'These upstarts can give us a lot of trouble is they are not stopped.'

'The youth must settle matters among themselves,' Dr Kamal said, with suppressed anger.

Several young men began adjusting the public address system on the stage and then one of them began to speak. He gave the audience a preliminary brief account of how he and several friends had been drawn to the politics of the People's Movement in Cape Town and had decided to form a branch in the city.

'Mr Chairman, I object!'

Salim Hoosein stood up.

'May I remind you that there is a political organisation here, the Orient Front. You may have heard of it.'

'I have heard of it. But I feel that there is a need for a different kind of political organisation. Let me explain . . .'

Several voices interjected:

'What do you mean?'

'Is the Front dead?'

'Are you issuing a challenge?'

The speaker pleaded for order and said that members of the audience would have ample time to ask questions later.

'Mr Chairman, are you trying to smear the Orient Front?' Salim Rashid shouted.

Before he could answer several voices accused the new group of trying to divide the Indian people in their liberatory struggle. Then someone boomed:

'Uncivilised Indians, don't you know anything about meeting procedure.'

Dr Kamal jumped up from his seat and turning in the direction of the voice said:

'I strongly object to the defamatory slur cast upon us by someone in the hall. For his information, I must state that we Indians are among the most civilised races of mankind, a people with a glorious culture . . .'

'Well, that is quite plain to all,' a cynical voice near him said. 'Why don't you keep quiet and let the meeting get on?'

He sat down, his body quivering. The rebuke stung him with such ferocity that for a moment, while standing, he had felt his body reeling as if he was about to plunge down a vertiginous height. His dignity and status had suffered a humiliating reduction. What compelling force had made him jump up from his seat and expose himself to the audience and identify himself, so it seemed to him, with the opponents of the new political group? He had come as an observer—a delusion he had managed to sustain until a few moments ago—but now he had become involved in their dispute. He should have stayed at home. The new group seemed to have many more sympathisers than he had calculated; people were taking them seriously. If the Youth League was defeated . . . he did not have time to complete the thought as, with the volume of the public address system amplified, the Chairman continued:

'Some of us felt that what we lacked here was a political body that would unify the oppressed. We are convinced that any organisation opposed to racialism should not have a racial structure, such as that of the Orient Front, or the African Front . . .'

Salim Rashid leapt from his seat.

'Don't insult the Orient Front! Don't insult the organisation founded by the great Mahatma Gandhi!'

He rushed forward and immediately members of the Youth League rose to follow their leader. Friends and sympathisers of the new group in the audience, shocked at first by the sudden threat of violence, jumped up from their seats and pressed towards the front to join the fray.

There was uproar and panic. Women screamed. The stage became a mass of seething, pushing, wrestling, punching, shouting combatants. From the rear of the hall one had the impression that players in a drama were involved in a mock battle.

Someone ran out of the hall to telephone the police.

When Salim Rashid leapt from his seat shouting his battle cry and rushing forward, Dr Kamal had experienced a sharp conflict within. There was the urge to flee from the violence he had contrived, and there was a petrifying inertia compelling him to remain and witness the battle. He stayed, trapped by indecision and the ambiguity of his political commitment, but when he saw the opposition's determination to fight the Youth League members, he rose from his seat. He took a few hurried steps, reached the foyer and stopped at the door. Policemen with truncheons and guns rushed past him into the hall.

Driven by a turbid amalgam of curiosity, fear and bewilderment, Dr Kamal re-entered the hall and watched horrified at the new dimension added to the battle. Then he fled. The centre of his being that had been in turmoil during the past few weeks seemed to be undergoing a kind of physical rot and together with this feeling he sensed the approaching storm of reproach and stigma that would engulf him. He reached his car. As he drove homewards Salim Rashid's words—aroused flaming furies—pursued him:

'Don't insult our organisation. . .'

Protista

Dambudzo Marechera

There was a great drought in our region. All the rivers dried up. All the wells dried up. There was not a drop of water anywhere. I lived alone in a hut next to the barren fig-tree which had never been known to have any fruit on it. Now and then it would show signs of being alive but these always withered and were carried away by the relentless winds from the south-east which were dry and dusty and would sting into the very coolness of our minds. Those winds, they were fierce and scathing and not a drop of moisture was left.

My hut was on a slight rise on the shoulder of the Lesapi Valley. The valley was red and clayey and scarred with drought fissures from the burning sun and the long cold nights when I lay awake thinking of Maria the huntress who had one morning taken down her bows and arrows and had gone out into the rising sun and had never been seen again. But before she left she had drawn a circle in red chalk on the wall by my bed and said: 'If the circle begins to bleed and run down the wall that means I am in danger. But if it turns blue and breaks up into a cross then that means I am coming home.'

The drought began the very day she left me. There was not a green blade of grass left. There was not a green leaf of hope left; the drought had raised its great red hand and gathered them all and with one hot breath had swept all the leaves into a red dot to the pencil-line of the horizon where Maria had last been seen taking aim with her bow and arrow at a running gazelle.

And twelve long lean years had passed by somehow.

I still had three more years to serve. I had been exiled to this raw region by a tribunal which had found me guilty of various political crimes. Maria had been my secretary and my wife and had for long endured the barren fire of exile with me. And the sun burnt each year to cinders that darkened the aspect of the region. I began to forget things. My dreams still clung defiantly to the steel wire of old memories which I no longer had the power to arrange clearly in my mind. My imagination was constantly seared by the thought of water, of thirst, of dying barren and waterless and in the grave to be nothing but dehydrated 'remains'. It was not so much forgetting as being constantly preoccupied with the one image of water. And water in my mind was inextricably involved with my thoughts about Maria, about my own impotence, about the fig-tree, and about the red soil of the Lesapi Valley. The years of my life that had gone were so much time wasted, so little done, so many defeats, so little accomplished; they were years I would have preferred to forget if they did not in themselves contain my youth and the only time Maria and I had been happy together. And now, disjointed, disconnected, they came back to me unexpectedly and with such a new grain in them that I hardly recognised them for what they were. There was the story my father had told me, when I was barely six years of age, about the resilience of human roots: a youth rebelling against the things of his father had one morning fled from home and had travelled to the utmost of the earth where he was so happy that he wrote on their wall the words 'I have been here' and signed his new name after the words; the years rolled by with delight until he tired of them and thought to return home and tell his father about them. But when he neared home his father, who was looking out for him, met him and said 'All this time you thought you were actually away from me, you have been right here in my palm.' And the father opened his clenched hand and showed the son what was written in this hand. The words—and the very same signature—of the son were clearly written in the father's open palm: 'I have been here.' The son was so stunned and angry that he there and then slew his father and hung himself on a barren fig-tree which stood in the garden. I dreamed of this story many times, and each time some detail of it would change into something else. At times the father would become Maria the huntress; the son would be myself; and the fig-tree would become the tree just outside my own hut. But sometimes the son would become Maria and I would be the father whose clenched hand contained everything that Maria was.

The scarred hand of exile was dry and deathlike and the lines of its palm were the waterless riverbeds, the craters and fissures of dry channels scoured out of the earth by the relentless drought. My own hands, with their scars and callouses and broken fingernails, sometimes seemed to belong not to me but to this exacting punishment of exile. And yet they had once tenderly held Maria to me; and she had been soft and warm and wild and demanding in these very same hands. These hands that now were part of the drought, they had once cupped the quickening liquids of life, the hearty laughter of youth, the illusory security of sweet-smelling illusions. These hands that now were so broken, they had once tried to build and build and build a future out of the bricks of the past and of the present. These hands that had never touched the cheek of a child of my own, they were now utterly useless in the slow-burning furnace of the drought whose coming had coincided with Maria's going away from me.

Her arms were long and thin and the fingers were long and finely moulded though her nails, like mine, had long since lost their natural lustre and had become broken and jagged. And she was gentle, fiercely so, for she knew her great strength. She was a head taller than I and her long full legs sometimes outstrode me when we went out for a walk in the Lesapi Valley. I had named the valley Lesapi after my birthplace where once I had learned to fish, to swim and to lie back into the soft green grass and relax, with my eyes closed and my head ringing with the cawing of the crows and the leisurely moo of cows grazing on Mr Robert's side of the river, where it was fenced and there was a notice about trespassers. And in the summer the white people held rubber-boat races on the river and sometimes I was allowed to watch them swirling along in the breezy hold of the river. But somebody drowned one day and my father told me not to go down to the river any more because the drowned boy would have turned into a manfish and he would want to have company in the depths of the waters. Water was good, but only when it did not have a manfish in it. My first nightmare was about a white manfish which materialised in my room and licked its great jaws at me and came towards my bed and said: 'Come, come, come with me', and it raised its hand and drew a circle on the wall behind my head and said, 'That circle will always bleed until you come to me.' I looked at his hand and the fingers were webbed, with livid skin attaching each finger to another finger. And then he stretched out his index finger and touched my cheek with it. It was like being touched by a red-hot spike; and I cried out, but I could not hear my own voice: and they were trying to break down the door, and I cried out louder and the wooden door splintered apart and father rushed in with a world war in his eyes. But the manfish had gone; and there was a black frog squatting where he had been. The next day the medicine-man came and examined me and shook his head and said that an enemy had done it. He named Barbara's father, and my father bought strong medicine which would make what had been done to me boomerang on Barbara's father. They then made little incisions on my face and on my chest and rubbed a black powder into them, and said that should I ever come near water I must say to myself: 'Help me, grandfather.' My grandfather was dead, but they said that his spirit was always looking and watching over me. They made a fire and cast the black frog into it, and the medicine man said he would seed its ashes in Barbara's father's garden. But he could do nothing about the circle on the wall, because although I could clearly see it no one else could. Shortly after this, my eyes dimmed a little and I have had to wear spectacles since then; at the time, however, it only made the little circle jump sharply at me each time I entered my room. The spot where the manfish had touched me swelled with pus, and mother had to boil water with lots of salt and then squeeze the pus out and bathe it with the salted water; after that it healed a little, and ever since I have always had a little black mark there on my face. Soon afterwards Barbara's father went mad and one day his body was fished out of the river by police divers who wore black fishsuits. There were various abrasions on his face and the body was utterly naked, and something in the river seemed to have tried to eat him—there were curious toothmarks on his buttocks and his shoulders had been partially eaten; the hands looked as though something had chewed them and tried to gnaw them from the arms.

Every morning, when the sun rose, there was a fine mist in the valley, and the interplay of the sun's rays on it created fantastic images within the mist. And they invariably looked like people I had once known. The shapes within the mist were somewhat formless, and yet with such a realistic solidity to them that I could never quite decide what to think. I had named the valley to give it the myths and faces of moments in my own life. But as the years went by, the waterless valley— paralysed by the cramping effects of an overwhelming oppression—emitted its own symbolic mists which overpowered my own imagination, and at last so erupted with its own smoke and fire and faces and shapes that I could not tell which valley was the real Lesapi. I had been physically weakened by the great shortage of water and the shortage of food. Besides, I had never been very strong. And this eerie region which was so stricken by the sun seemed to have a prodigious population of insects: flies, mosquitoes, cicadas, spiders, and scorpions. The cicadas were good to eat; the rest tormented me with their sudden stinging. The massive difference between the temperature of the days and the temperature of the nights was also a severe torture. And the manner in which I had been brought up was not calculated to cramp and stifle the imagination; rather my imagination has always been quick to the point of frightening me. All this made the valley come out alive at my very doorstep. The circle which Maria had drawn on the wall seemed alive; it was in constant motion, changing colour, breaking and rearranging itself into a cross, moving again into a circle and bleeding and running down the wall till I cried in my sleep. It seemed I was in many places at one and the same time; my sleeping and waking had no difference between them. There was a sharp but remote flame of pain inside my head; it seemed I was not so much talking to myself as talking to the things of that valley.

I woke up one morning and at once felt in myself that something was wrong. I could not move; I could move neither my body nor my hands nor my feet. At first I thought something had in the night strapped me down to the ground, but I could feel no bonds binding me. When I realised what had happened I almost cried out—but held my breath because there was no one to hear me. Not only had my hair grown into the floor like roots, but also my fingers and my toes and the veins and arteries of my body had all in my sleep grown into the earth floor. I had been turned into some sort of plant, I thought. And as soon as that thought seared through my head I immediately could feel that my skin had turned into bark. It has happened at last, I said to myself. As I did so I noticed that the circle on the wall had begun to bleed and was running down the wall: something had happened to Maria. I could not feel my eyes, nor my ears, but, strangely, I could see and I could hear. I do not know how long I lay there; nor what days or weeks passed as I lay there fighting back the feverish delirium that soon swamped me. And I was staring fixedly at Maria's life bleeding on the wall; and stared at it so much that I could see nothing else but that red circle bleeding slowly down the wall.

It was like sleeping with one's eyes open.

The footsteps outside had stopped at my door and I could hear heavy breathing. The roof rattled a little as the south-east wind swept by. And then the breathing stopped. The wind stopped too, and the roof did not rattle any more. It suddenly dawned on me that the footsteps were actually inside me; they were my old heart beating, my old things come home. The door had not opened, but I could see her clearly. She was mere bones, a fleshless skeleton, and she was sitting on a tree-trunk. I was the tree-trunk. I do not know how long she sat there. She was weeping; clear tears, silvery and yet like glass, coming out of the stone of her eyeless sockets; and her small gleaming head rested in the open bones of her palms, whose arms rested lightly on her knees. And she held between her front teeth a silver button which I recognised: I had years before bought her a coat which had buttons like that. It was the sight of her forlornly chewing that button which filled me with such a great sadness that I did not realise that my roots had been painlessly severed and that what was left to do was to bind my wounds and once more—but with a fresh eye—walk the way of the valley. The roof was rattling once more; the south-east winds were singing a muffled song through the door. And those horrid footfalls retreated until their distant echo beat silently in my breast.

After that, the sun never came up. I do not know where it had decided to go. Perhaps it fell into the sea where the great manfish lives. Anyway, the night did not come either; it had retreated to the bedrock of the deepest sea where the great manfish came from. There was in the sky so much of its face that even the stars had grown vicious and turned into menfish. And they all wanted company; they were all hungry for me, thirsty for me. But I kept a careful watch and always chewed the silver button, because that alone can keep them away. Yesterday I met Barbara's father in the valley:

'I'll get you in the end, you rascal!' he screamed.

But I bit the silver button and turned myself into a crocodile and laughed my great sharp teeth at him.

He instantly turned himself into mist, and I could only bite chunks of air. While I was cursing him, a voice I did not recognise said:

'You thought it was all politics, didn't you?'

But there was no one there.

I sneered:

'Isn't it?'

And I sullenly turned myself back into human shape. I had decided to write all this down because I do not know when the stinking menfish will get me. Maria, if ever you find this—my head is roaring with fever and I scarcely know what I have written—I think the menfish are out to undermine my reason—if ever you find this—I think Barbara's father is coming to get me and the sky and the earth and the air are all full of monsters like him and me—like him—I wish I had been able to give you a child—my head!—all grown-ups are menfish, but remember perhaps there is still a chance that the children—my head!

I have been a manfish all my life. Maria, you did well to leave me. I must go.

The Coffee-Cart Girl

Ezekiel Mphahlele

The crowd moved like one mighty being, and swayed and swung like the sea. In front, there was the Metropolitan Steel Windows Ltd. All eyes were fixed on it. Its workers did not hear one another: perhaps they didn't need to, each one interested as he was in what he was saying—and that with his blood. All he knew was that he was on strike: for what? If you asked him he would just spit and say: 'Do you think we've come to play?'

Grimy, oily, greasy, sweating black bodies squeezed and chafed and grated. Pickets were at work; the law was brandishing batons; cars were hooting a crazy medley.

'Stand back, you monkeys!' cried a black man pinned against a pillar. 'Hey, you black son of a black hen!'

The coffee-cart girl was absorbed in the very idea of the Metropolitan Steel Windows strike, just as she was in the flood of people who came to buy her coffee and pancakes: she wasn't aware of the swelling crowd and its stray atoms which were being flung out of it towards her cart until she heard an ear-splitting crash behind her. One of the row of coffee-carts had tipped over and a knot of men fallen on it. She climbed down from her cart, looking like a bird frightened out of its nest.

A woman screamed. Another crash. The man who had been pinned against the pillar had freed himself and he found himself standing beside the girl. He sensed her predicament. Almost rudely he pushed her into the street, took the cart by the stump of a shaft and wheeled it across the street, shouting generally, 'Give way, you black monkeys.' Just then a cart behind him went down and caved in like matchwood.

'Oh, thank you so much, mister!'

'Ought to be more careful, my sister.'

'How can I thank you! Here, take coffee and a pancake.'

'Thank you, my sister.'

'Look, they're moving forward, maybe to break into the factory!' When next she looked back he was gone. And she hadn't even asked him his name: how unfriendly of her, she thought . . .

Later that winter morning the street was cleared of most people. The workers had gone away. There had been no satisfactory agreement. Strikes were unlawful for black people anyhow.

'Come back to work, or you are signed off, or go to gaol,' had come the stock executive order. More than half had been signed off.

It was comparatively quiet now in this squalid West End sector of the city. Men and women continued their daily round. A dreary smoky mist lingered in suspension, or clung to the walls; black sooty chimneys shot up malignantly; there was a strong smell of bacon; the fruit and vegetable shops resumed trade with a tremulous expectancy; old men stood Buddha-like at the entrances with folded arms and a vague grimace on their faces, seeming to sneer at the world in general and their contemptible mercantile circle in particular; and the good earth is generous enough to contain all the human sputum these good suffering folk shoot out of their mouths at the slightest provocation. A car might tear down the cross-street and set up a squall and weep dry horse manure so that it circled in the air in a momentary spree, increasing the spitting gusto . . .

'Hullo.'

'Hullo, want coffee?'

'Yes, and two hot buns.'

She hardly looked at him as she served him. For a brief spell her eyes fell on the customer. Slowly she gathered up the scattered bits of memory and unconsciously the picture was framed. She looked at him and found him scanning her.

'Oh!' She gave a gasp and her hand went to her mouth. 'You're the good uncle who saved my cart!'

'Don't uncle me, please. My name is Ruben Lemeko. The boys at the factory call me China. Yours?'

'Zodwa.'

His eyes travelled from her small tender fingers as she washed a few things, to her man's jersey which was a faded green and too big for her, her thin frock, and then to her peach-coloured face, not well fed, but well framed and compelling under a soiled black beret. As he ate hungrily she shot a side-glance at him occasionally. There was something sly in those soft, moist, slit eyes, but the modest stoop at the shoulders gave him a benign appearance; otherwise he would have looked twisted and rather fiendish. There was something she felt in his presence: a repelling admiration. She felt he was the kind of man who could be quite attractive so long as he remained more than a touch away from the contemplator; just like those wax figures she once saw in the chamber of horrors.

'Signed off at the Metropolitan?'

'Hm.' His head drooped and she could read dejection in the oily top of his cap. 'Just from the insurance fund office.' She pitied him inwardly; a sort of pity she had never before experienced for a strange man.

'What to do now?'

'Like most of us,' looking up straight into her eyes, 'beat the road early mornings just when the boss's breakfast is settling nicely in the stomach. No work, no government papers, no papers, no work, then out of town.'

'It's hard for everybody, I guess.'

'Ja.'

'I know. When you feel hungry and don't have money, come past here and I'll give you coffee and pancake.'

'Thanks, er—let me call you Pinkie, shall I?'

'Hm,' she nodded automatically.

He shook her hand. 'Grow as big as an elephant for your goodness, as we say in our idiom.' He shuffled off. For a long time, until he disappeared, she didn't take her eyes off the stooping figure, which she felt might set any place on fire. Strange man Pinkie thought idly as she washed up.

China often paused at Pinkie's coffee-cart. But he wouldn't let her give him coffee and pancakes for nothing.

'I'm no poorer than you,' he said. 'When I'm really in the drain pipes you may come to my help.'

As she got used to him and the idea of a tender playfellow

who is capable of scratching blood out of you, she felt heartily
sorry for him; and he detected it, and resented it and felt sorry
for her in turn.

'Right, Pinkie, I'll take it today.'

'You'll starve to death in this cruel city.'

'And then? Lots of them starve; think of this mighty city,
Pinkie. What are we, you and me? If we starved and got sick
and died, who'd miss you and me?'

Days when China didn't come, she missed him. And then
she was afraid of something; something mysterious that
crawls into human relations, and before we know it it's there;
and because it is frightening it does not know how to
announce itself without causing panic and possibly breaking
down bonds of companionship. In his presence she tried to
take refuge in an artless sisterly pity for him. And although he
resented it, he carried on a dumb show. Within, heaven and
earth thundered and rocked, striving to meet; sunshine and
rain mingled; milk and gall pretended friendship; fire and
water went hand in hand; tears and laughter hugged each
other in a fit of hysterics; the screeching of the hang-bird
started off with the descant of a dove's cooing; devils waved
torches before a chorus of angels. Pinkie and China panicked
at the thought of a love affair and remained dumb.

'Pinkie, I've got a job at last!'

'I'm happy for you, China!'

'You'll get a present, first money I get. Ach, but I shouldn't
have told you. I wanted to surprise you.' He was genuinely
sorry.

'Don't worry, China, I'll just pretend I'm surprised really,
you'll see.' They laughed.

Friday came.

'Come, Pinkie, let's go.'

'Where to?'

'I'll show you.' He led her to the cheapjack down the street.

'Mister, I want her to choose anything she wants.'

The cheapjack immediately sprang up and in voluble catar-
acts began to sing praises upon his articles.

'All right, mister, let me choose.' Pinkie picked up one
article after another, inspected it, and at last she selected a
beautiful long bodkin, a brooch, and a pair of bangles. Naidoo,

the cheapjack, went off into rhapsodies again on Pinkie's looks when China put the things on her himself, pinning the bodkin on her beret. He bought himself a knife, dangling from a fashionable chain. They went back to the coffee-cart.

From this day onwards, Naidoo became a frequent customer at Pinkie's coffee-cart. He often praised her cakes and coffee. Twice at lunch-time China found him relating some anecdotes which sent Pinkie off into peals of laughter.

'Where you work, my prend?' asked Naidoo one day. He was one of the many Indians who will say 'pore-pipty' for 'four fifty', 'pier foms' for 'five forms', 'werry wital' for 'very vital'.

'Shoe factory, Main Street.'

'Good pay?'

'Where do you find such a thing in this city?'

'Quite right, my prend. Look at me: I was wanted to be a grocer, and now I'm a cheapjack.'

'I'm hungry today, Pinkie,' China said one day. He was clearly elated over something.

'It's so beautiful to see you happy, China, what's the news?'

'Nothing. Hasn't a man the right to be jolly sometimes?'

'Of course. Just wondered if anything special happened.'

He looked at her almost transparent pink fingers as she washed the coffee things.

'Hey, you've a lovely ring on your finger, where's the mine?'

Pinkie laughed as she looked at the glass-studded ring, fingered it and wipe it.

'From Naidoo.'

'What?'

'It's nothing, China. Naidoo didn't have any money for food, so he offered me this for three days' coffee and cakes.' She spoke as if she didn't believe her own self. She sensed a gathering storm.

'You lie!'

'Honestly China, now what would I be lying for?'

So! he thought, she couldn't even lie to keep their friendship: how distant she sounded. His fury mounted.

'Yes, you lie! Now listen Pinkie, you're in love with that cheapjack. Every time I found him here he's been damn happy with you, grinning and making eyes at you. Yes, I've watched him every moment.'

He approached the step leading into the cart.

'Do you see me? I've loved you since I first saw you, the day of the strike.' He was going to say more, but something rose inside him and choked him. He couldn't utter a word more. He walked slowly; a knife drawn out, with a menacing blade, pointed towards her throat. Pinkie retreated deeper into her cart, too frightened to plead her case.

At that very moment she realised fully the ghastliness of a man's jealousy, which gleamed and glanced on the blade and seemed to have raised a film which steadied the slit eyes. Against the back wall she managed to speak.

'All right, China, maybe you've done this many times before. Go ahead and kill me; I won't cry for help, do what you like with me.'

She panted like a timid little mouse cornered by a cat. He couldn't finish the job he had set out to do. Why? He had sent two men packing with a knife before. They had tried to fight, but this creature wasn't resisting at all. Why, why, why? He felt the heat pounding in his temples; the knife dropped, and he sank on to a stool and rested his head on the wall, his hands trembling.

After a moment he stood up, looking away from Pinkie. 'I'm sorry, Pinkie, I pray you never in your life to think about this day.'

She looked at him, mystified.

'Say you forgive me.' She nodded twice.

Then she packed up for the day, much earlier than usual.

The following day China did not visit Pinkie; nor the next. He could not decide to go there. Things were all in a barbed wire tangle in his mind. But see her he must, he thought. He would just go and hug her; say nothing but just press her to himself because he felt too mean even to tell her not to be afraid of him any more.

The third day the law came. It stepped up the street in goose-march fashion. The steel on its heels clanged on the pavement with an ominous echo. It gave commands and everything came to an end at once. Black man's coffee-cart was not to operate any more in the city. '. . . Makes the city look ugly,' the city fathers said.

For several days China, unaware of what had happened, called on Pinkie, but always found the coffee-carts empty and deserted. At last he learned everything from Naidoo, the cheapjack.

He stepped into her coffee-cart and sat on the stool.

He looked into the cheerless pall of smoke. Outside life went on as if there had never been a Pinkie who sold coffee and pancakes.

Dare he hope that she would come back, just to meet him? Or was it going to turn out to have been a dream? He wondered.

We'll meet in town, some day, China thought. I'll tell her all about myself, all about my wicked past; she'll get used to me, not be afraid of me any more . . .

And still he sat in the coffee-cart which was once Pinkie's all through the lunch-hour . . .

Snapshots of a Wedding

Bessie Head

Wedding days always started at the haunting, magical hour of early dawn when there was only a pale crack of light on the horizon. For those who were awake, it took the earth hours to adjust to daylight. The cool and damp of the night slowly arose in shimmering waves like water and even the forms of the people who bestirred themselves at this unearthly hour were distorted in the haze; they appeared to be dancers in slow motion, with fluid, watery forms. In the dim light, four men, the relatives of the bridegroom, Kegoletile, slowly herded an ox before them towards the yard of MmaKhudu, where the bride, Neo, lived. People were already astir in MmaKhudu's yard, yet for a while they all came and peered closely at the distorted fluid forms that approached, to ascertain if it were indeed the relatives of the bridegroom. Then the ox, who was a rather stupid fellow and unaware of his sudden and impending end as meat for the wedding feast, bellowed casually his early morning yawn. At this the beautiful ululating of the women rose and swelled over the air like water bubbling rapidly and melodiously over the stones of a clear, sparkling stream. In between ululating all the while, the women began to weave about the yard in the wedding dance; now and then they bent over and shook their buttocks in the air. As they handed over the ox, one of the bridegroom's relatives joked:

'This is going to be a modern wedding.' He meant that a lot of the traditional courtesies had been left out of the planning for the wedding day; no one had been awake all night preparing diphiri or the traditional wedding breakfast of pounded meat and samp; the bridegroom said he had no church and did not care about such things; the bride was six months pregnant and showing it, so there was just going to be a quick marriage ceremony at the police camp.

'Oh, we all have our own ways,' one of the bride's relatives joked back. 'If the times are changing, we keep up with them.' And she weaved away ululating joyously.

Whenever there was a wedding the talk and gossip that preceded it were appalling, except that this time the relatives of the bride, Neo, kept their talk a strict secret among themselves. They were anxious to be rid of her; she was an impossible girl with haughty, arrogant ways. Of all her family and relatives, she was the only one who had completed her 'O' levels and she never failed to rub in this fact. She walked around with her nose in the air; illiterate relatives were beneath her greeting—it was done in a clever way, she just turned her head to one side and smiled to herself or when she greeted it was like an insult; she stretched her hand out, palm outspread, swung it down laughing with a gesture that plainly said: 'Oh, that's you!' Only her mother seemed bemused by her education. At her own home Neo was waited on hand and foot. Outside her home nasty remarks were passed. People bitterly disliked conceit and pride.

'That girl has no manners!' the relatives would remark. 'What's the good of education if it goes to someone's head so badly they have no respect for the people? Oh, she is not a person.'

Then they would nod their heads in that fatal way, with predictions that one day life would bring her down. Actually, life had treated Neo rather nicely. Two months after completing her 'O' levels she became pregnant by Kegoletile with their first child. It soom became known that another girl, Mathata, was also pregnant by Kegoletile. The difference between the two girls was that Mathata was completely uneducated; the only work she would ever do was that of a housemaid, while Neo had endless opportunities before her—typist, bookkeeper, or secretary. So Neo merely smiled; Mathata was no rival. It was as though the decision had been worked out by circumstance because when the families converged on Kegoletile at the birth of the children—he was rich in cattle and they wanted to see what they could get—he of course immediately proposed marriage to Neo; and for Mathata, he agreed to a court order to pay a maintenance of R10.00 a month until the child was twenty years old. Mathata merely smiled too. Girls like her offered no resistance to the approaches of men; when they lost them, they just let things ride.

'He is of course just running after the education and not the manners,' Neo's relatives commented, to show they were not fooled by human nature. 'He thinks that since she is as educated as he is they will both get good jobs and be rich in no time . . .'

Educated as he was, Kegoletile seemed to go through a secret conflict during the year he prepared a yard for his future married life with Neo. He spent most of his free time in the yard of Mathata. His behaviour there wasn't too alarming but he showered Mathata with gifts of all kinds—food, fancy dresses, shoes and underwear. Each time he came, he brought a gift and each time Mathata would burst out laughing and comment: 'Ow, Kegoletile, how can I wear all these dresses? It's just a waste of money! Besides, I manage quite well with the R10.00 you give every month for the child . . .'

She was a very pretty girl with black eyes like stars; she was always smiling and happy; immediately and always her own natural self. He knew what he was marrying—something quite the opposite, a new kind of girl with false postures and acquired, grand-madame ways. And yet, it didn't pay a man these days to look too closely into his heart. They all wanted as wives, women who were big money-earners and they were so ruthless about it! And yet it was as though the society itself stamped each of its individuals with its own particular brand of wealth and Kegoletile had not yet escaped it; he had about him an engaging humility and eagerness to help and please that made him loved and respected by all who knew him. During those times he sat in Mathata's yard, he communicated nothing of the conflict he felt but he would sit on a chair with his arms spread out across its back, turn his head sideways and stare at what seemed to be an empty space beside him. Then he would smile, stand up and walk away. Nothing dramatic. During the year he prepared the huts in his new yard, he frequently slept at the home of Neo.

Relatives on both sides watched this division of interest between the two yards and one day when Neo walked patronisingly into the yard of an aunt, the aunt decided to frighten her a little.

'Well aunt,' she said, with the familiar careless disrespect which went with her so-called, educated, status. 'Will you make me some tea? And how's things?'

The aunt spoke very quietly.

'You may not know it, my girl, but you are hated by everyone around here. The debate we have going is whether a nice young man like Kegoletile should marry bad-mannered rubbish like you. He would be far better off if he married a girl like Mathata, who though uneducated, still treats people with respect.'

The shock the silly girl received made her stare for a terrified moment at her aunt. Then she stood up and ran out of the house. It wiped the superior smile off her face and brought her down a little. She developed an anxiety to greet people and also an anxiety about securing Kegoletile as a husband—that was why she became pregnant six months before the marriage could take place. In spite of this, her own relatives still disliked her and right up to the day of the wedding they were still debating whether Neo was a suitable wife for any man. No one would have guessed it though with all the dancing, ululating and happiness expressed in the yard and streams of guests gaily ululated themselves along the pathways with wedding gifts precariously balanced on their heads. Neo's maternal aunts, all sedately decked up in shawls, sat in a select group by themselves in a corner of the yard. They sat on the bare ground with their legs stretched out before them but they were served like queens the whole day long. Trays of tea, dry white bread, plates of meat, rice, and salad were constantly placed before them. Their important task was to formally hand over the bride to Kegoletile's maternal aunts when they approached the yard at sunset. So they sat the whole day with still, expressionless faces, waiting to fulfil this ancient rite.

Equally still and expressionless were the faces of the long column of women, Kegoletile's maternal aunts, who appeared outside the yard just as the sun sank low. They walked slowly into the yard indifferent to the ululating that greeted them and seated themselves in a group opposite Neo's maternal aunts. The yard became very silent while each group made its report. Kegoletile had provided all the food for the wedding feast and a maternal aunt from his side first asked:

'Is there any complaint? Has all gone well?'

'We have no complaint,' the opposite party replied.

'We have come to ask for water,' Kegoletile's side said, meaning that from times past the bride was supposed to carry water in her in-law's home.

'It is agreed to,' the opposite party replied.

Neo's maternal aunts then turned to the bridegroom and counselled him: 'Son, you must plough and supply us with corn each year.'

Then Kegoletile's maternal aunts turned to the bride and counselled her: 'Daughter, you must carry water for your husband. Beware, that at all times, he is the owner of the house and must be obeyed. Do not mind if he stops now and then and talks to other ladies. Let him feel free to come and go as he likes . . .'

The formalities over, it was now time for Kegoletile's maternal aunts to get up, ululate and weave and dance about the yard. Then, still dancing and ululating, accompanied by the bride and groom they slowly wound their way to the yard of Kegoletile where another feast had been prepared. As they approached his yard, an old woman suddenly dashed out and chopped at the ground with a hoe. It was all only a formality. Neo would never be the kind of wife who went to the lands to plough. She already had a well-paid job in an office as a secretary. Following on this another old woman took the bride by the hand and led her to a smeared and decorated courtyard wherein had been placed a traditional animal-skin Tswana mat. She was made to sit on the mat and a shawl and kerchief were placed before her. The shawl was ceremonially wrapped around her shoulders; the kerchief tied around her head—the symbols that she was now a married woman.

Guests quietly moved forward to greet the bride. Then two girls started to ululate and dance in front of the bride. As they both turned and bent over to shake their buttocks in the air, they bumped into each other and toppled over. The wedding guests roared with laughter. Neo, who had all this time been stiff, immobile, and rigid, bent forward and her shoulders shook with laughter.

The hoe, the mat, the shawl, the kerchief, the beautiful flute-like ululating of the women seemed in itself a blessing on the marriage but all the guests were deeply moved when out of the crowd, a woman of majestic, regal bearing slowly approached the bride. It was the aunt who had scolded Neo for her bad manners and modern ways. She dropped to her knees before the bride, clenched her fists together and pounded the ground hard with each clenched fist on either side of the bride's legs. As she pounded her fists she said loudly:

'Be a good wife! Be a good wife!'

Reflections in a Cell

Mafika Gwala

Yesterday I felt like tearing the bars down with my bare hands. Now all that rage in me has been cooled by Mr Shezi's visit. Although I'm no VIP—actually I hate VIPs—this visit has done me good. I've been brought to my senses about that lousy term 'being a social problem'. Am I being a social problem? Hell, someone will have to tell him that guys like me are not going to be bullied by suckers like Mr Shezi into 'being a man'.

I can't be the man they want, sit in the pub the whole afternoon, fill my stomach with beer and talk a lot of tribal politics; or wear a suit, drive an American car and talk a lot of American-English garbage. Someone will have to tell Mr Shezi, I won't. All I can do is thump him. Man, I've got no time to open my mouth for suckers.

But I'm no social problem, really. I simply want to lead a full life without them sticking their dirty noses into it all the time. I'm sure Shezi is taking my story to those powdered bitches who'll be discussing it at some tea party. How they waste their time. They should be walking through their gardens and cuddling their pet dogs, that's what they're fit for.

I can still remember Mrs Lane at Eshowe. That's where I was sent to for juvenile deliquency, but I don't remember being a juvenile and this the suckers don't know. One day I was being exhibited to an overseas tourist who had just popped in to see how things were with us darkies. Hell, we were all glum. That's the game we played whenever any of these peacocks dared step into our yard. Several questions were fired at me (perhaps because I was the sulkiest). And I was not prepared to answer. I couldn't hold out any longer when this touring peacock says, 'Just think how much your parents could have done for you.' I snarled at her, that's what I did, and told her I didn't care a damn about them. (Of course I was lying.) It just popped into my mind. When they granted us the kind favour of leaving, I heard Mrs Lane whispering to the visitor, shrugging her shoulders, 'Well, you see what a grey pride the Zulus have?' Maybe I should have kept my sour mind to myself. How could she compare me to a bloody Zulu boy of 'them' days? They all want us to be Zulu boys and then they can pour their pity on us.

And Shezi doesn't know this bit. I've known Shezi for five years now. He still harps on the old gospel—'Be a man', when all he knows is carrying his big bag around and playing it to the professional standard. I was sent to the reformatory just for refusing to go to school. I mean, if a man gets bored to death, turning pages and cramming passages, he is not doing anything criminal. I wonder if you ever felt like that anytime. Me, the history class drove me mad, all that big talk on the Great Trek and inventions and the teacher only saying after each passage, 'You can imagine how things were in those days.' Nothing more than that, as if it were the only thing he caught at Training College.

I was doing JC at the time I started hanging around the local shop and killing time at the cinema. The serials were great in those days. I remember not missing one episode of 'Fu Manchu', you should know that one, 'The Drums of Fu Manchu'. My old lady bought me over with fags and bio-start so I could sell her dagga. I used to shayisa most of the stuff at the Scala. As long as my old barlly was out, I was boss at home, and the old lady did her washing on the Berea. Then one day the old barlly, my father, got even with me for a lousy ten bob. I don't know how he gripped me in the first place because I was having him for a long time. Hard luck, I think, but you see I don't believe in luck. The next day I was taken to the Police Station at Mayville. And the lynchings, whe-ew!

'Send him to the reformatory, Mr Zondi,' a lady with mannish looks advised my father, scrutinising me as if I was a soldier on parade. The trousers still hurt my backside.

The boys did not ill-treat me at Eshowe. I only had to turn my eyes devilishly to make a man skrik and I kept them off. Then I met Joey. A guy with sharp features and a coldness that made others always feel his presence. Joey had been to Kimberley, there's a reformatory there too. And he had skipped it and managed to reach Sharpeville, his home town.

'Imagine coming home to find the place deserted and people weeping all over. I don't know what brought me home, to find my mother and father dead—gunfire. Just when I was going to make a fresh start and find myself a smart job and help my parents if they didn't send me back to the reformatory—I had it all planned. But there I was, with no place to go. Back into the streets of Vereeniging I went, bag snatching again and this is where I am today.' Joey was reading a Hadley Chase. Here was a guy with no guilt or pity for himself, or anything like that. We made a serious twosome, Joey and I.

'But sonny, I want to get into real money now, big money, in a grand style, like they do in here.' He hammered at the paperback cover. Novels were not allowed I should add. Newspapers and magazines were mostly in Afrikaans.

We got on very well, Joey and me: he telling me about Bloody Monday and fast life on the Reef and me loading it all on him, Mkhumbane—that's Cato Manor—Mayville and Durban life. He just wrote to me lately. He told me he's gone big time. I never believed he would try it. Anyway, I wish him all the best.

Back from the reformatory, I was a different man. In a way. And I couldn't stand any shit from another man. My family now lived at Kwa-Mashu. Shezi drove me home, that's how we met. This chap has been pestering me all along when I happen to 'waai' in.

The reception at home was cold. With mum and dad separated, I had to move away from the old barlly. The best thing for me was to walk out. Besides, a man couldn't stand the dull life at the new township, people not knowing one another. But the real reason was a term in jail.

I was new at Kwa-Mashu and a total stranger at home, except when my brother at University came home weekends. My father even told my kid brothers to keep an eye on me. Me a thief and the black sheep of the family. After three days I found a shebeen a street below my home. I had four rands in my pocket—I needn't say where I got it from. At first I called for Zulu beer, then a nip of cane and beer again. Hell, I was high. Now there were a few blokes jiving in the room, with two girls. Another one walked in, school-going (she had a uniform on and carried books). This one I hooked onto without much effort. It began with small talk. This was her sister's place and they were from the Reef. We switched to fly-taal; Joey had got me used to it. The girl jived so beautifully. The boys' jail had made me rusty.

Then one of these guys looks at me with contempt. I'm not used to that. With me it's a tooth for a tooth and I gave the swine a dirty look too. One to make him cringe inside. He then tried to impress with his Zulu tsotsi-taal. I ignored him. She wasn't pretty, but she wasn't bad either—she could be had. Now I can't remember if the guy caught up with what we were saying or if it was plain jealousy. For I heard him say, 'Here we roll "Kom Van's".' He thought I was a Transvaler. To drown him in more anger I offered the girl a drink. She had refused theirs, see. Hell, and the bloody thing swallowed it like it was lemonade. A stiff tot, eh.

Since it was getting late I finished my cane and made plans to lay her. I was to wait outside, at the gate. The chaps followed me. Something told me to hop it, but then I wouldn't see the girl. The same sucker asked me where I lived.

'You got no right to ask me that, boeda.'

'Do you still leave him?'

One of them advanced. And within a few seconds I had taken out my McGregor. He hit out. Missed. I pinned him below his right shoulder. His friends fell back. I drilled another hole on his back and pulled out fast. I got six strokes for that, my first trouble with the law. After a six-month sentence for theft, I pushed off to Verulam. My granny's place.

I still wonder why my dad sent Shezi to check me. The fellow doesn't care. And it's almost seven weeks since I got pitched up here. Funny. As long as Dougie doesn't talk I'm not squealing about it either. This bloke's got guts and because I admire his guts I'm not going to betray him. A man values his gun and I like him for it.

It's a long rambling story about how I got into this dark cell.

Verulam is a small town so I soon learned my way about it. The guys here were nice, I mean nice. They could still afford a good laugh, something I had missed at the reformatory and at home. I got on easily with them when they saw I could light a pipe neatly and serve it equally well. My reading habits raised

me a bit too. With a little discrimination I could level off the big
guns without anybody biting his lips. That kind of thing. With
me a bloke could spin a coin as best he could without a stir. My
position was snug with these hustlers; we were all big battlers.
Rolling a zol with mango leaves became my special interest
too.

That's how I came to know Dougie. He had flunked his JC
having learned busting a pipe and dodging school. We were in
the same boat, like. I was one guy with whom he could enjoy
scientific talk, as he put it. The guy is some kind of genius; the
way he loves maths and engineering! He'll talk of ship building
and aircraft designing. Look at Tex, he'll say, the bastard
never uses his brains. I don't know how he got through his
nine. Dougie failed to conceal his dislike for 'educated bastards'. I hope this doesn't hurt you. You don't look the sort of
guy to be easily hurt. His brother was a doctor, actually he still
is, and they failed to see eye to eye. That could be the reason.
Or maybe his brother is a bastard: there are so many of them.

Anyway, that has nothing to do with me being here.

We were gambling at Brime's tearoom. The whole crowd
was there. A goofed lad with spitting cotton on the sides of his
mouth—Sammy, who walked as if there was red-hot iron on
the ground and could imitate any singer with his guitar and
singing—Elvis, the Beatles. Otis Redding. Ray Charles. With
him any number could win and that's the only reason anybody
liked him. There was Micky Two who had switched from
being a shoe-shine boy to washing taxis at the rank; Jack, who
always had a football magazine shoved in the back pocket of
his Levi's and dreamed of playing like Pèle—good as he is he
drinks too much. And Jay Singh, a hawk-eyed and serious
chap who made a point of seeing every Steve McQueen picture
and talking about it. Eveyone called him the Kid for his
neck-or-nothing gambling habits. No man could lose like him.

And there was Alec, just from 'inside' after pulling eighteen
months for a small part in an armed robbery. Alec was a new
man now; the way he held the fag, the way he forced an angry
look onto his baby-face. If there is anything good he inherited
from his prison term, that's honesty. I mean honesty, not the
blind honesty of the Bible. For the first time I heard him say
'no' when he wasn't sure of something. His loud-mouthed

expression had also gone. He moved in a dignified manner, like a soldier who has won his first stripe in the army and has to play up to his new station.

There were many more guys there that afternoon. I can't count them all. There was also Ismail, a dirty fat slob and a police pimp.

Dougie's jalopy rattled onto the scene.

'Move one side, you sloppy head.' Dougie could bully anybody when he felt like it.

'Laaities, give us some air.' He was bellowing at a group of interested boys.

'What's all this conglomeration?' That was Micky Two.

'Congregation Micky, not conglomeration,' someone poked in.

'Conglomeration, who's talking of congregations? You can't tell me fuck-all, I go for big terms. I was once a tea-boy for a fuckin' lawyer, what are you telling me a snaai like you.' The atmosphere was already hot; Sipho, a very rash gambler had lost two rands and his face was changing. But there was Dougie to handle him in case he tried funny tricks, so the game was safe. Jay was already pawning his jacket, just to lay a bet.

'Some ganja if a man smaaks any.' Dougie had several parcels in his hands.

'Ketna?' Harry wanted to buy.

'You know I slaat my zol bob-a-time, and I don't slaat jinks.'

'Ok, gimi one kaatjie.' That's the way a man had to deal. You had to try one kaatjie first, that was the law of the game—know a guy's stuff well before you plunge in.

'Hell, Rooies, gimi another four kaatjies and keep the change.' He gives him a fifty-cent piece.

Dougie passed the start onto me. 'We go it fifty-fifty.' Though he liked me, today Dougie was being unusually kind. We gambled and lost.

'You bloody gulls, fonky makes donky.' I was on the rocks, so we had to back out.

'You want to catch a nigh?' Dougie asks me. I say sure. Who doesn't like a nigh? That man must be a fool.

'Let's beat it then—Greenwood Park.' By this time I knew most of Dougie's connections at Greenwood and at Sydenham. He was their merchant, exchanging dagga for pinched stuff like copper, goods from the docks or any other gadget that brought him cash. I dived into the jalopy.

'No time to tune,' he told me as we parked before one big house. 'All you do is make eyes at her while I'm talking, if she raises her voice then I know you're in. I'll just slip into the next room with her sister. She won't let you tune, too stuck up.' So we ducked into the house. It worked out to the last figure.

'The jerries came here looking for Emmanuel. What's up?' the elder sister, the thin one with broad hips, asked Dougie.

'He hasn't registered for military training for all I know. And I can't understand why they want us "coloureds" to fight for them, it's their little business they want to solve, not ours.'

We left after dusk. After a few more stops we headed for Verulam.

'I've got some thick soup for us two here Mike. Can I trust you?'

'You never doubted me in the first place, at least you didn't show it. But why buy me over with a fuck?'

'To open the deal in a clean way.'

'The deal is settled.' I guess I had no choice. Friendship for friendship. Dougie took from the back seat that queer parcel he had taken from the big house. Wrapped in brown paper was an FN rifle, two brownies and a .33.

There are customers in the reserves, I'm sure. You know the draads. We parted and I took the stuff home. I had reliable connections who could take the articles for the price I named. Two more days to go and I get rid of the bloody stuff. Buried them, that's what I did. I can afford to tell you this because you don't look like a pimp. You are an honest man, I can see it in your eyes. Too damned good to get into a fighting mood. You can't smack a fly, that is the trouble with you, man. Honest and educated, not many educated guys are honest these days.

So I had two days to go. Exactly two days. I was sure of my cards. Monday, and the cash comes in.

But on Sunday morning I was in for a surprise. Just coming from my girl's place and my granny's waiting for me. 'Police were looking for you. They got Dougie. You still causing trouble? I thought you had changed.' I had changed, but a man is always a victim of circumstance.

'Circumstance! When you let it come into your way?' Granny was boiling. She forgets that once you're in, you're in for keeps. And I'm one guy who'll play the game to the end.

They nabbed me the following day. My blind move: I shouldn't have gone to the pictures. For the whole day I wasn't home on Sunday and I slept out at another girl's place. A man was moving on a moving target, see. Next day I thought I should straighten my limbs and the cinema was the natural thing for me. To blues my problems away in action. Maybe it's because I've got no ear for music. Too sentimental for me.

Even the film wasn't worth half the risk, that Costa Nostra type where the fellow joins them when he fails to beat them. A very lousy thing for a man who wants to live. Live, man, live. I hadn't checked the display casement. I just burrowed in.

When I sneaked out there was a white jerry at the door. Someone even said they were looking for a terrorist, silly things people can say at times about others. I can't figure myself being labelled a terrorist. Idea now was to walk slowly until I reached the opposite side of the street. I had gone past the cop; he didn't know me. That bastard Ismail—I have a feeling he burned my boats—the way he cast his dirty eyes at me when the jerry pounced on me. Then they brought me here in a dark van.

Two cops, darkies, snatched me out of the van. Giants, they set me thinking of a Tarzan colour film, smelling of an artificial jungle.

'*Nou praat, jou kaffer, daai boesman het alles belui.*' Which boesman? The man was off his nuts. I know that dirty old trick. I put the see-saw together; even if Dougie had talked I had to deny it at first, to be one better than the buggers. Then why is he not here, or show me his statement, I mean his confession. Nothing. If he hasn't talked, he must be shading someone at the end of the line. The thin girl with broad hips only knew Dougie and me. Poor thing. She must have failed to stand the slaps.

'*Meneer, ek is nie 'n kaffer.*' First step towards baffling his jerry mentality. The bastard senses my defiant innocence as I pretend to study his callousness with self-pity. I have my conclusions about him and this he fails to see. They all fail.

'You're not going to co-operate with us?' Big jerry again.

'Where are the guns?'

'I'm co-operating, and you don't seem to appreciate my effort. That is the difference.' Of course, I'm lying.

'*Hy gaan praat dié donner, Meneer.*' A hefty Indian in plain clothes collars me. Buster you're wrong. Never mind the torture.

Do I have to go through the fistings and the kickings that first day? And the torture every third day since I'm here? I don't want to go in for contravening the Official Secrets Act or for Perjury, if you're going to report my story. And I wonder when will you get out of here.

I also hate taking oaths and abiding by them like a blaring sheep. There is a time when I've felt I couldn't take any more, but something told me, don't take it lying down and you've won.

'So, kaffer, you're not talking?' The officer with moustaches like Hitler's is trying to bully me. None of that 'kaffer' stunt with me.

'Well, my boy, since we can't get a thing out of you, we shall have to scratch it out. Is that what you want?' They all try to be innocent once you show your teeth. As if he cares a brass farthing for what I want.

'I want to get out of here, I know nothing about guns, can't your brains soak that in?' My turn to be aggressive now. One thing I learned from Joey is that a man should stick by his guns. And why are they so worried about three, four miserable guns? Why, you tell me?

Because I'm sure Dougie swore by all the gods, I had nothing to do with guns. So is he. That man's got guts. Guts to wipe me clean. Or they would have shown him to me. As long as he keeps his trap shut, I'm silent. Those two bitches. We shouldn't have got involved in this. Like I said, one can't blame female weakness at times.

'Well, I sympathise with you. You were helping a friend and you forgot it was criminal,' the Hitler is saying. They sympathise and yet tighten the screws: this I've learned.

'We are keeping you till you speak truth.' Truth, what truth? And the torture. All I know is because I didn't break that day, they'll keep on wasting their bloody time and breath.

So today they are turning the heat on me. Again. And again.

I'll just have to pin my concentration on one thing: I'm not talking.

By the way, don't you think it's strange being shut in here with you? There are two possibilities, either you're a pimp or I've won. A clear win, that's what I think it is.